THE LAMB AND THE TIGER

From Peacekeepers to Peacewarriors in Canada

In *The Lamb and the Tiger*, Stanley R. Barrett explores the broad implications of Canada's transformation from a peacekeeping to a war-making nation during the Conservative Party's recent decade in power. Funds were poured into the Canadian Forces, and a newly militarized nation found itself entrenched in conflicts around the globe. For decades, Canada had played a leading role in UN peacekeeping, and when the Cold War ended the prospect of international harmony was infectious. Yet in short order hostilities erupted in the failed states of Rwanda, Somalia, and the Balkans; terrorism – including 9/11 – raised its head; and Iraq and Afghanistan became war zones. In the face of these immense challenges, the UN was dismissed by its opponents as irrelevant.

Structured around an anti-war perspective, *The Lamb and the Tiger* critically examines the ageless genetic and more recent cultural explanations of war and includes a close look at the impact of war and right-wing politics on women and Indigenous peoples. *The Lamb and the Tiger* encourages Canadians to think about what kind of military and what kind of country they really want.

STANLEY R. BARRETT is a Professor Emeritus in the Department of Sociology and Anthropology at the University of Guelph.

UTP Insights

UTP Insights is an innovative collection of brief books offering accessible introductions to the ideas that shape our world. Each volume in the series focuses on a contemporary issue, offering a fresh perspective anchored in scholarship. Spanning a broad range of disciplines in the social sciences and humanities, the books in the UTP Insights series contribute to public discourse and debate and provide a valuable resource for instructors and students.

Books in the Series

- Stanley R. Barrett, *The Lamb and the Tiger: From Peacekeepers to Peacewarriors in Canada*
- Peter MacKinnon, *University Commons Divided: Exploring Debate and Dissent on Campus*
- Raisa B. Deber, *Treating Health Care: How the Canadian System Works and How It Could Work Better*
- Christina D. Rosan and Hamil Pearsall, *Growing a Sustainable City? The Question of Urban Agriculture*
- Jim Freedman, *A Conviction in Question: The First Trial at the International Criminal Court*
- John Joe Schlichtman, Jason Patch, and Marc Lamont Hill, *Gentrifier*
- Robert Chernomas and Ian Hudson, *Economics in the Twenty-First Century: A Critical Perspective*
- Stephen M. Saideman, *Adapting in the Dust: Lessons Learned from Canada's War in Afghanistan*
- Michael R. Marrus, *Lessons of the Holocaust*
- Roland Paris and Taylor Owen (eds.), *The World Won't Wait: Why Canada Needs to Rethink Its International Policies*
- Bessma Momani, *Arab Dawn: Arab Youth and the Demographic Dividend They Will Bring*
- William Watson, *The Inequality Trap: Fighting Capitalism Instead of Poverty*
- Phil Ryan, *After the New Atheist Debate*
- Paul Evans, *Engaging China: Myth, Aspiration, and Strategy in Canadian Policy from Trudeau to Harper*

THE LAMB AND THE TIGER

From Peacekeepers to Peacewarriors in Canada

Stanley R. Barrett

UNIVERSITY OF TORONTO PRESS
Toronto Buffalo London

© University of Toronto Press 2018
Toronto Buffalo London
utorontopress.com
Printed in Canada

ISBN 978-1-4875-0341-3 (cloth)
ISBN 978-1-4875-2263-6 (paper)

Printed on acid-free, 100% post-consumer recycled paper with
vegetable-based inks.

Library and Archives Canada Cataloguing in Publication

Barrett, Stanley R., 1938–, author
The lamb and the tiger : from peacekeepers to peacewarriors in
Canada / Stanley R. Barrett.

(UTP insights)
Includes bibliographical references and index.
ISBN 978-1-4875-0341-3 (cloth). – ISBN 978-1-4875-2263-6 (paper)

1. War and society – Canada.   2. Militarism – Canada.   3. Peacekeeping
forces, Canadian.   4. Canada. Canadian Armed Forces.   I. Title.
II. Series: UTP insights

HM554.B37 2018   303.6'60971   C2018-904970-7

University of Toronto Press acknowledges the financial assistance to its
publishing program of the Canada Council for the Arts and the Ontario
Arts Council, an agency of the Government of Ontario.

Canada Council   Conseil des Arts
for the Arts   du Canada

ONTARIO ARTS COUNCIL
CONSEIL DES ARTS DE L'ONTARIO
an Ontario government agency
un organisme du gouvernement de l'Ontario

Funded by the   Financé par le
Government gouvernement
of Canada   du Canada

Canada

*Dedicated to the memory of
Virgil Duff
Inspirational Editor
at the University of Toronto Press*

Contents

Preface

Who would believe that in the short span of a decade a nation's brand, its defining characteristics, indeed its heart and soul, could be transformed to such an extent that it became barely recognizable at home and abroad? Nowhere were the changes in Canada more evident and dramatic than in the military and political realms. Peacemaking gave way to war-making, and the country's political culture lurched sharply to the right.

Although I have been deeply disturbed by these changes, interpreting them as an assault on the precious qualities that have made our multicultural nation so decent, there is nothing in my background that led inevitably to this attitude. I grew up in a lower-middle-class family of six brothers in an Ontario village. This was Progressive Conservative country, and my father, a talented carpenter with his own small business, was fiercely independent and self-reliant, adamantly opposed to unions and government interference. He also was a member of the Orange Order, then a force to be reckoned with in the Protestant enclaves of rural Ontario.

My only memories of the Second World War were the ritual burning of an effigy of Hitler at the village fairgrounds when the war ended, whispered gossip about neighbours whose sons had lost their lives while serving overseas, food shortages during the war, and the excitement in the village when a star hockey player returned from the battlefields unharmed and once again led the local team to glory.

Primary school passed by in an aura of dreamy distraction, but secondary school was a beast. I failed grade 10 and grade 12 and was earmarked for the factory floor until a close friend persuaded me to accompany him to a university in the United States (why I was accepted remains a mystery; maybe someone in admissions had a wicked sense of humour). The following year I transferred to Acadia University in Nova Scotia, graduating in 1963 with a BA in English literature and philosophy.

In retrospect it is stunning to recall just how naive and uneducated I still was at that time, as well as the extent to which the conservative world view of the village of my youth continued to shape my own. For example, when I began to teach in a secondary school in Igbo (or Biafran) territory in Nigeria under the auspices of Canadian University Service Overseas (CUSO) after graduation, a story appeared either in *Time* or *Newsweek* (I can't remember which) pointing out that the United States was home to a huge underclass of impoverished citizens. When my students asked me how this could be in the richest and most powerful country in the world, I was at a loss for words. It never crossed my mind to question the capitalist system, let alone its racist underbelly.

It was in Africa where my first experience of war unfolded. On a hitchhiking trip with a pal across the middle of the continent from Nigeria to East Africa, we arrived in Sudan and discovered that Khartoum was engulfed by a civil war. Demolished tanks cluttered that fabled city, with piles of rubble and furtive civilians around every corner.

Just over three years later, I was back in Nigeria doing research for a PhD in anthropology, this time among the Yoruba. By then the Biafran War, set in motion by Igbo secessionist aspirations, was in full swing. Roadblocks in Yoruba territory were everywhere. On one occasion a soldier singled me out and declared I was a spy for Biafra. He was drunk and threatened to shoot me on the spot. Fortunately I had learned enough of the local language to disarm his hostility. Embracing me, he proclaimed that I was his "tight" friend (in the context, an ironic choice of words) and waved me cheerily on my way. A few months later the Biafran War ended. Concerned about the fate of my former students, I travelled there and witnessed the devastation: bomb-cratered roads, empty food stalls in the markets, and the aimless and stunned demeanour of the survivors. At the same time I learned that several of my former students had been killed during the war. It was these first-hand experiences, no doubt almost trite in comparison to what so many victims around the globe have faced, that gave rise to a conviction that has become firmer with each passing decade: war is an abomination. This brings me back to Canada. The recent political efforts to turn it into a militarized nation in the service of narrow Western interests dictate one of the most profound and relevant questions in this study: what kind of military and what kind of country do we want?

John McMurtry, a philosopher and former colleague at the University of Guelph who has inspired so many of us, generously critiqued my preliminary outline and offered his encouragement. His powerful monograph, *Understanding War* (1988), is featured in chapter 7. I have relied heavily on the extensive work of another Guelph colleague, Edward Hedican, a recognized authority on First Nation communities. Discussions with Terry Dokis, a professor at Nipissing University who had been one of my very first students long ago, persuaded me that Aboriginal Canadians had an important place in this study; probably more than he realized, it was his subtle mind that alerted me to many of the issues on which I have focused.

Two of the most remarkable individuals who have become my friends in recent years have military backgrounds, one a veteran of the Second World War, the other a high-ranking officer in the British services. If most members of the military came close to matching their level of decency, no other institution could rival it. Equally impressive are two of my nephews whose collective knowledge and experience about the central themes of this study – especially military and security issues – makes me look like an amateur. If they ever read this book, I hope that they will remember that blood is thicker than water and appreciate that their aged uncle has provided them with a splendid opportunity to display their capacity for kindness and compassion. Along the way a number of individuals expressed interest in and commented wisely on this project, especially Bridget Lytton-Minor, Neil MacKinnon, Georgia Marman, George McLeod, Rob Pontsioen, Melodie Pritchard, and Bernard Senault.

This book very definitely benefited from the critical evaluations of the outside readers arranged by the publisher, as well as from the close attention to detail exhibited by my first editor there, Doug Hildebrand. Kaye once again exceeded the call of duty at every stage of this project, and it would be no exaggeration to state that to a considerable extent this is her book too.

THE LAMB AND THE TIGER

From Peacekeepers to Peacewarriors in Canada

chapter one

Introduction

When I began to reflect on the transformation of Canada from peacekeepers to warriors, or Orwellian "peacewarriors," mirroring the tendency in recent years to blur the distinction between warmaking and peacemaking, William Blake's intriguing poem *The Tiger* (or Tyger) popped into my head:

> Tiger, tiger burning bright
> In the forests of the night ...
> Did He who made the lamb make thee?

For most of the period from the end of the Second World War until the first decade of the twenty-first century, an era dominated by Liberal governments, Canada was a lamb, its reputation as a peacekeeper celebrated both at home and abroad. With the election of Stephen Harper's Conservative Party in 2006, accompanied by a rapid expansion and rebranding of the military as a fighting force, the lamb had mutated into a tiger, although the genetic seeds for the fearsome creature had been sown by Paul Martin's short-lived Liberal administration.

Several excellent studies sharply critical of the shift in the Canadian military from peacekeepers to warriors, plus the wider ideology of the Conservatives, already exist, including McQuaig, *Holding the Bully's Coat* (2007), Nadeau, *Rogue in Power* (2011), and especially the perceptive portrayal of the militarization of Canada by McKay and Swift (2012). Of course, apologists for the military and the

Conservatives have not been twiddling their thumbs, particularly two prolific historians who enjoy the stature of public intellectuals: Jack Granatstein, *Whose War Is It?* (2007) and David Bercuson, *Significant Incident* (1996), plus their joint autopsy of the Canadian military mission in Afghanistan, *Lessons Learned* (2011). Drawn into the fray have been several well-known journalists, with Lawrence Martin, for example, making a case for peacekeeping and the Liberals (2010), and Paul Wells cosying up to the Conservatives (2013).

My angle into the debate about what kind of military we want and what kind of country we want (these are almost the same question) revolves around resistance – a theme with a long and rich history in anthropology. Opposition to a militarized Canada was substantial. In the decades following the Second World War there were periodic efforts by the international community to promote peace over war, and in Canada the military was starved and sidelined by unsympathetic governments. Yet within the past decade such has been the rise in the fortunes of the Canadian military, inspired no doubt by the horror of 9/11, that it sometimes has been lauded as the country's most important and respected institution.

Obstacles to a right-wing drift in the political realm were equally daunting: the entrenched liberal values of Canadians, especially robust support for the UN, a love affair with the peacekeeping tradition and welfare programs such as universal health care, and a dedicated commitment to minority rights. Yet the Conservative Party led by Stephen Harper managed to impose an ideology and political culture that lodged the nation within the orbit of the most extreme elements of America's Republican Party.

How did the military on the one hand and the Conservatives on the other surmount formidable barriers in the way of their ambitions? The first thing to point out is that their interests coincided; the Conservative agenda nourished the military, and a strengthened military reinforced the Conservatives. Men and women in the military were less than enamoured with peacekeeping. They were trained for war, and as one high-ranking soldier who had served in Afghanistan told me, his troops craved to be tested on the battlefield, to be "blooded." The Conservatives poured funds into the military, set it loose in war zones, while at the same time mothballing its peacekeeping role.

In turn, the newly muscular military's adventures abroad in hot spots like Afghanistan contributed to the government's success in nudging the nation away from the UN and towards narrower Western institutions and interests such as NATO and American foreign policy. These forays into enemy territory also enhanced the government's capacity to prioritize security over citizen rights and freedoms, and the accompanying culture of fear provided a cover for what appeared to be an onslaught on the nation's democratic traditions. Certainly there were additional factors in the Conservative Party's victory such as the weakened and fragmented opposition parties, and the clever, disciplined, and relentless partisan leadership of Harper himself. Yet it was the reciprocal benefits of the military and the Conservatives, possibly more than anything else, that enabled each of them to triumph in the face of resistance.

In this study the lamb and the tiger will be employed as metaphors. The lamb: soft power, peace, internationalism, tolerance, relativism, and compromise. The tiger: hard power, aggression, provincialism, intolerance, absolutism, and ideological rigidity.

It may be wondered why realism hasn't been added to the list attached to the tiger, and idealism to that of the lamb. After all, people in favour of hard power are often labelled realists, while soft power advocates are more likely to be described as idealists. Yet ideals and values animate the Conservative Party: individual rather than group rights, small rather than big government, liberty over justice, hierarchy over equality, and the associated belief that individuals – not society – are responsible for their achievements or lack of them in life. Conservatives also look favourably on the military virtues of loyalty, duty, discipline, fortitude, honour, and patriotism. Finally, there is their absolute faith in unbridled capitalism, along with the conviction that almost no greater harm can be saddled on people than to drag them into the clutches of the welfare bureaucracy.

Conservatives, then, possess a full-blown and coherent ideology, and they genuinely believe that their vision has the capacity to benefit not just the party faithful but indeed all Canadians. Of course, as the 2015 triumph of Justin Trudeau's Liberals proclaimed loud and clear, not everyone finds the Conservative dream enthralling. Although I have never belonged to a political party, I have spent a lifetime of study trying to understand and oppose inequality in all its forms, which is another way of stating that I am hardly neutral about the competing political ideologies. Indeed, if this modest study better equips Canadians to resist the more extreme forms of conservatism, I won't shed any tears.

I hasten to add that almost every effort will be made to balance my biases with a fair and accurate portrait of the conservative vision, albeit spiced up occasionally with a pinch of irony or satire. The risk, of course, is that if the praise is excessive, the study may end up as a recruitment magnet for the politics of privilege. How ironic that would be!

Part One provides a detailed description and analysis of the shift in Canada from peacekeepers to a fighting force. Part Two, with its deeper focus on the genetic and cultural basis of war, serves as a conceptual foundation for Parts One and Three. In the latter, case studies are sketched out to reveal the impact of war and politics on women and Aboriginals. Although there is much to criticize about the genetic and cultural frameworks, not only do they overlap to a remarkable degree, but they also resonate profoundly with the world views of the politicians and military elite and their enthusiastic supporters who were enthralled with the prospect of a militarized nation. Tracking the themes of this study from cover to cover is the shadow of the counter-Enlightenment. All around the globe there are signs that the Enlightenment values of rationalism, empiricism, universalism, and secularism are being dislodged by xenophobia, ethnocentrism, parochialism, nationalism, and religious fervour. This is a social movement with momentum, and despite the Liberal triumph at the polls in 2015, the legacy of the Age of Reason in Canada remains vulnerable.

In the chapters that follow I shall attempt to cast some light on a number of questions that have puzzled me from the moment I began to think about this project, including this sample:

Military

1.   Why (and how) the switch from peacekeepers to warriors?
2.   Why war: genetics, culture, both or otherwise?

3. Can a country be considered great and enjoy international respect without an impressive military?
4. Is the military the pivotal institution in a nation? Should it be?
5. Is the military Canada's most pro-American institution?
6. Is it true that the last people who want war are soldiers, or at least combat veterans?
7. Is the history of a nation primarily the history of war?
8. Should nations that celebrate their soldiers as the ultimate heroes, the cream of the crop, be applauded or regarded as borderline barbaric and a threat to the world community?

Politics

1. Is Western democracy on its last legs, in danger of being bowled over by the authoritarian version of democracy that prevails in much of ascendant Asia?
2. In view of Harper's attacks on Parliament and the rights and freedoms of citizens, should he be labelled a genius for recognizing the above and placing Canada on the wave of the future?
3. Why has talk about disarmament and world peace dwindled to a whisper?
4. Why have so few top-notch world leaders, statesmen who inspire, emerged since the Second World War?
5. Is inequality the root of most societal problems?
6. Is the UN doomed, or is there still hope that it can live up to its mandate?
7. Is human progress in the sense of enabling all peoples around the globe to realize their potentials in an atmosphere devoid of oppression a child's dream? Is there a limit to human progress? Have we already reached it, and are we now in danger of regressing?
8. The xenophobic focus on "barbaric cultural practices" seemed to be the final nail in the coffin of the Conservative Party during the 2015 election. Will the day ever come when racist-tinged politics, reminiscent of a previous era, triumph in Canada?

part one

Disputed Visions

chapter two

Peaceful Kingdom

There can be no doubt about the identity of the Canadian or the international incident that set the tone for the nation's love affair with UN peacekeeping operations. The man was Lester B. Pearson, and the incident was Egyptian President Nasser's decision in 1956 to nationalize the Suez Canal, prompting Britain and France to join forces in order to protect their interests. Their bizarre plan was to arrange for Israel to attack Egypt and then to invade under the guise of defending Israeli troops. While the specific goal was to retake control of the Suez Canal, the more general one was to overthrow the Nasser regime.

Pearson, a committed internationalist who had been a member of the Canadian delegation involved with the founding of the United Nations, and who had played a central role in the formation of NATO, was in 1956 minister for external affairs in St Laurent's Liberal government. In an address to the UN General Assembly, where he had served as president in 1952, Pearson introduced an innovative solution to the conflict: the positioning of an international force between the belligerents. Although the peacekeeping venture was a great deal more convoluted than this brief account suggests, the bottom line is that it worked. The British and French relinquished their colonial ambitions in Egypt, the Israelis retreated to their recently acquired homeland, war was averted, and Pearson, much to the delight of Canadians, was awarded the 1957 Nobel Peace Prize.

While the Suez Canal incident marked the beginning of what became known as classic UN peacekeeping, characterized by consent and impartiality, with force resorted to only in self-defence, a handful of other missions preceded it. In Palestine and Korea in 1948 and Kashmir in 1949, UN observers monitored elections, ceasefires and troop withdrawals.[1] The 1950–3 Korean War certainly was far removed from peacekeeping. In a bloody prelude to the Cold War, the UN sanctioned an American-led force to confront communist North Korea; among the 26,000 Canadian troops that fought alongside the Americans, 516 lost their lives.

From 1956 to 1990, Canada participated in about forty UN peacekeeping missions around the globe. In fact Canada joined every UN mission over that period except one involving Angola in 1989. No other nation, large or small, could match that record, or the sheer number of Canadians (125,000) who donned blue helmets and died in service (120). On 9 August 1974, nine Canadian peacekeepers were killed when Syrian forces shot down their aircraft. The Canadian Association of Veterans in United Nations Peacekeeping eventually selected 9 August as our nation's Peacekeeping Day.

In the decades following Pearson's triumph, Canadians embraced peacekeeping as if it were part of their DNA. They enthusiastically supported the humanitarian efforts of men and women in uniform and prided themselves as the little nation that was unrivalled in its commitment to world harmony – a sort of domestic version of American exceptionalism. Monuments celebrating peacekeeping have been erected in various cities, and peacekeeping symbols have appeared on Canadian currency. In 1988 the Nobel Peace Prize was awarded to UN peacekeepers collectively. The Canadian government recognized the significance of the award by commissioning a monument in Ottawa called Reconciliation. Its symbols of peace stand in contrast to The Response nearby, the National War Memorial for the fallen in the First World War.

By the late 1950s nuclear disarmament was in the air. In 1958 two prominent Americans presented their ideas for total disarmament known as the Clark-Sohn Plan (see McQuaig 2007, 183). A year later both Britain and the Soviet Union responded by tabling disarmament proposals in the UN. In 1960 the Ten Nation Disarmament Committee was formed consisting of five Eastern Bloc countries (including the Soviet Union) and five Western Bloc countries (including the United States and Canada). Its purpose was to negotiate complete disarmament. In 1961 the United States and the Soviet Union issued a joint statement confirming their commitment to the momentous initiative. Then the wheels fell off. The Cuban Missile Crisis in 1962, with the threat of nuclear war, pulverized all talk about disarmament and held captive a nervous world. I was an undergraduate at the time and vividly recall that some students wondered if there were even any point to studying.

It eventually became obvious that the Cuban Crisis was merely one incident in a trend. Every time peace talks and disarmament proposals seemed to be making progress, a new international crisis, whether by accident or design, erupted, and the world once again was on a war footing.

Undoubtedly the greatest opportunity to establish world peace emerged when the Berlin Wall was torn down in 1989. But before that happened, there was another initiative that was altogether strange. In 1986 Reagan and Gorbachev put their heads together during an informal meeting in Iceland and astonished humanity by announcing their agreement for total disarmament and a nuclear-free world. The agreement soon was scuttled, partly because of Reagan's dreamy insistence on Star Wars, and partly because the hawks in the American Republican Party and the military coaxed him back in line.

Joining the hawks apparently was Reagan's soulmate, Margaret Thatcher (Runciman 2015). Her re-election prospects in Britain hinged on her conviction that a nuclear arsenal was not only here to stay but in fact was the indispensable deterrent to a third world war. If the Gorbachev-Reagan initiative was not aborted, she would be vulnerable to the disarmament-promoting peaceniks in the rival political parties. At a quickly arranged meeting with Reagan at Camp David, Thatcher made her case. Reagan, no doubt already softened up, capitulated.

The demolition of the Berlin Wall signalled the end of the Cold War and provided the UN with the jolt of energy that it had been waiting for since the 1950s. The slogan of the moment was "the peace dividend," the idea that a new world had emerged, one that was finally ready to implement the lofty goals of peace, security, and freedom from oppression and poverty for all humanity.

The hopes for a revitalized and effective UN were articulated in a potent document entitled "An Agenda for Peace," prepared by the secretary-general of the UN, Boutros Boutros-Ghali (1992), an Egyptian diplomat and expert on international law. "Agenda for Peace" was quite forward-looking in that it fully recognized how the world had changed, unleashing new expressions of conflict such as fanatic nationalism, ethnic rivalry, failed states, and terrorism. It was also realistic in its awareness that Chapter VI in the UN Charter, based on the classic peacekeeping model of consent, impartiality, and limited force, had become less appropriate than Chapter VII, which authorized aggressive UN military responses.

"Agenda for Peace" also contained its fair share of controversy. It warned about the dangers of climate change: "A porous ozone shield could pose a greater threat to an exposed population than a hostile army." If this later raised the ire of global warming sceptics in the American Republican Party and in Canada during Harper's reign, so too must have the secretary-general's assertion that the basic causes of conflict throughout the globe are "economic despair, social injustice and political oppression."

Most controversial of all, at least in terms of the philosophy of the UN, may have been the document's comments about the principle of consent. Here there was a huge contradiction. On the one hand there was the recognition that sovereign states will continue to be the basic building blocks of international order. On the other hand, Boutros-Ghali wrote that the days of "absolute and exclusive sovereignty" were over. In other words, consent, when circumstances warranted it, was shelved. This opened the door to UN-backed military forays in future hotspots such as the Balkans, Libya, Syria, Somalia, and Afghanistan. It may also have paved the way for the Canadian-backed initiative, Responsibility to Protect (R2P), with the attendant moral quagmire regarding who decides what states should be violated and whose interests should prevail.

While the primary aim of peace advocates during the Cold War was total disarmament, especially the eradication of nuclear weapons, a related goal was to bolster the UN's effectiveness by providing it with its own military force (and possibly a police force as well). From early in his career as a statesman, Pearson was in favour of such a force, and eventually Presidents Kennedy and Clinton (see McQuaig 2007, 183 and 193) came on board. Boutros-Ghali in "Agenda for Peace" portrayed the creation of a military and police capacity for the UN as essential, but when he requested member states to commit troops to a standing force, few bothered to reply. He got the same reaction when he asked member nations to provide needed equipment for peacekeeping such as vehicles and generators that could be stockpiled at UN facilities; or failing that to set aside such equipment in their own countries for potential UN operations.

Prime Minister Brian Mulroney was in office when "Agenda for Peace" was released to the public, and he must have supported it because Canadian officials contributed to the preparation of this clarion call for peace. His successor, Jean Chrétien, like Pierre Trudeau before him, was not enamoured with the military and put his own stamp of approval on the UN document.

In 1997, four years after Chrétien's government had achieved power, Canada joined several other countries that decided to buck the disinterest of the international community by establishing their own joint but limited UN military force. Dubbed Stand-by High Readiness Brigade (SHIRBRIG), it was briefly mobilized by the UN in peacekeeping ventures before fading from memory.

Another notable Canadian initiative for peacekeeping was the brainchild of two graduate students, Erika Simpson and Peter Langille. Inspired by the dividend for peace, they came up with the imaginative idea of converting the abandoned Cornwallis Naval Base in Nova Scotia into a centre to train peacekeepers from around the globe. With the support of the Chrétien government, in 1994 the Pearson Peacekeeping Centre was born, with additional chapters in Halifax, Montreal, and Ottawa. Funding for the Centre was divided between the Department of National Defence (DND) and the Canadian International Development Agency (CIDA).

As it will be shown in much more depth in the next chapter, the Canadian military establishment had been less than enthusiastic about "Agenda for Peace," and that same attitude prevailed in relation to the Pearson Centre; a steady barrage of criticism questioned both its necessity and legitimacy. As it turned out, the Chrétien government was no match for its military. The anticipated mandate of hands-on training for peacekeepers was shelved, and in its place the centre was reduced to a talk forum, periodically producing commissioned papers.

In 2008 the Harper government closed the Cornwallis Centre and the Halifax and Montreal branches as well and moved all operations to Ottawa. By 2012 the Ottawa office continued to exist on paper, but funding had dried up, and a year later its doors shut for good. Perhaps that was just as well, because its raison d'être – training peacekeepers for real life missions abroad – was stillborn from the outset.

Just as the Cuban Missile Crisis shot down the promising disarmament talks, the peace dividend so cherished by the UN suffered a similar fate. Even before the "Agenda for Peace" was released, the 1991 Iraq War erupted. President George H.W. Bush was no fan of the UN and was especially hostile to a world body that dared to infringe on America's independence and power or question the moral right to protect and enjoy its disproportionate wealth. Mulroney, who took office committed to closer cooperation with the Americans and to strengthening the Canadian military, sent fighter jets and ships to the Iraq theatre.

Mulroney also embarked on a plan to significantly expand Canada's armaments industry, only to discover that the treasury could not support the price tag. His solution was to turn to the private sector. American companies were invited to establish branch plants alongside Canadian-owned ones (McQuaig 2007, 172–3). Trudeau had previously considered expanding the armaments industry but only under the ownership and control of Canadians; little came of his plan, possibly because of similar financial constraints, and maybe because his heart was not in the venture. Mulroney's tactic of mobilizing the private sector was quintessential conservative ideology in action. It can only be hoped that the Liberals were broad-minded enough to appreciate his gift to the nation.

The Iraq War was only the initial indication that the 1990s were fated to be a nightmare for the advocates of world harmony. Following on its heels were three new volatile zones that proved to be almost too much of a challenge for the international community: the civil wars in Rwanda, Somali, and the Balkans.

Rwanda

In 1993 Canada responded to a UN request to make available a commander for a peacekeeping operation in Rwanda by selecting Brigadier-General Roméo Dallaire for the job. By the time he was back on Canadian soil a year later he was a broken man, suicidal, suffering from post-traumatic stress disorder. There was little in Dallaire's previous life and career that prepared him for the sheer brutality of the unfolding genocide in Rwanda, its horrors eventually described in his own words in *Shake Hands with the Devil* (2004).

Born into a military family, his father had been a non-commissioned officer during the Second World War and his mother a Dutch war bride, Dallaire's first love was the military. For a period he was stationed in Germany with NATO forces. His advancement through the military ranks appears to have been impressive, but prior to assuming command of United Nations Assistance Mission for Rwanda (UNAMIR) he had no field experience as a peacekeeper, although his highly capable assistant and fellow Canadian, Brent Beardsley, had served in Cyprus.

Rwanda was a Chapter VI UN mission, which meant the absence of force except in self-defence. As Dallaire revealed in his book, he assumed command entirely confident that classic peacekeeping was appropriate for the mission. Then reality knocked him like a sledgehammer. Rwanda, a former Belgian colony, had been left with its resources plundered and its ethnic rivalries enflamed. When mass killing erupted, Dallaire was powerless. The UN had not provided even a fraction of the troops and equipment that might have enabled him to successfully intervene, even if the mission had been granted Chapter VII status.

Dallaire made a valiant but hopeless effort to persuade the rival ethnic leaders to agree to a ceasefire and began to give live interviews to the CBC and other media outlets in order to alert the world to the unfolding tragedy. In his words (2004, 333): "The media was the weapon I used to strike the conscience of the world and try to prod the international community into action." His pleas failed to move either the UN leadership or any of its powerful member states. The unthinkable result was that in the short span of 100 days, 800,000 Rwandans were butchered.

In retrospect, Dallaire arrived at the realization that Chapter VI of the UN Charter, or classic peacekeeping, was hopelessly outdated in the context of failed states. He maintained (2004, 514) that the genocide in Rwanda could have been prevented had adequate troops and firepower, and a mandate to deploy them, been authorized under Chapter VII. Yet as he explained, a more robust mission was not in the cards, because Rwanda lacked the resources to attract the big powers, nor was it a threat to the international order.

Dallaire lamented the tendency of world powers to bypass the United Nations in pursuit of their own self-interests and went as far as accusing the United States, Britain, and France of aiding and abetting the Rwandan genocide by turning blind eyes to it. Perhaps what is most surprising in view of his harsh experiences is that he did not end up despising the UN. He remained a believer in its contribution to global harmony and order, but only when its operations involved robust peacemaking rather than its weaker predecessor.

Another surprise was the fact that he singled out America as one of the culprits in the Rwandan disaster. As it will be shown in the next chapter, the prevalent attitude of the Canadian Forces towards America and its military is almost obsequious. But Dallaire apparently never went on training exercises or exchange with the American military, often a precondition to career mobility for Canada's soldiers.

Happily, Dallaire was eventually able to put his life back together. Concern and support for him across the country was enormous, capped by his appointment to the Canadian Senate (he resigned from this increasingly controversial body in 2014). Before turning to Somalia, the next failed state to be examined, a cruel question must be raised. Did UNAMIR fail because it was not a well-equipped Chapter VII operation, or must Dallaire, described by McKay and Swift (2012, 167) as "Canada's most famous, if tragic, peacekeeper," assume part of the blame? He himself (Dallaire 2004, 515) questions whether he was too inexperienced for the job. Then there is his comment about his personality (26): "I have often been criticized for being an 'emotional' leader, for not being macho enough." Was this sensitive, humanistic individual simply the wrong man for the job? Would a more hard-headed, even ruthless leader have been more effective? Is that generally the case in the vast majority of military missions?

Somalia

Both Rwanda and Somalia were regarded as failed states, and both had sufficient Canadian content to engage the interest of its citizenry. But whereas the storyline in Rwanda was the enormous carnage and suffering, and only tangentially Dallaire's tragic heroism, Somalia barged into Canadian consciousness primarily because of the startling atrocities committed by Canada's own soldiers.

The Somalia mission surfaced in 1992 when the Security Council imposed a complete arms embargo on the country. The subsequent U.S.-led intervention was authorized by the UN and soon transformed into a Chapter VII operation. This appeared to be entirely justified if the UN's ambition to provide humanitarian aid to a country ripped apart by heavily armed competing warlords had any prospect of success. Significantly, the mission did not enjoy the consent of the Somali people, probably an unattainable condition in the volatile setting.

The inside story of Canadian atrocities is effectively analysed by McKay and Swift (2012, 199–206). Two separate events stood out. In 1993 Canadian soldiers shot and killed two young Somali civilians who had broken through the security fence of the Canadian compound. From a military perspective, such action might appear to have been warranted; after all, the Somalis might have been terrorists. But as the facts emerged, it was learned that they were shot while running away. To make the optics even worse, apparently soldiers were in the habit of placing food and water near the fence in order to lure victims within firing range.

The second event was even more despicable. A sixteen-year-old Somali was caught in the act of theft in the Canadian camp. Within the hearing of dozens of soldiers, he was tortured so severely by his assailants that he ended up dead. Neither of these incidents would probably have become public knowledge except for the actions of an Army physician, Major Barry Armstrong. Driven presumably by an admirable grasp of ethics, he defied the subsequent cover-up by the military, as well as the tradition for people in uniform to close ranks when confronted with a threat to their club.

When these and other atrocities finally made the headlines back in Canada, the Chrétien government appeared reluctant to deal with the situation, but enraged public opinion demanded action. The Canadian troops that had been sent to Somalia served in the Airborne Regiment, often depicted as an elite, gung-ho fighting force, a surprising choice for a UN peacemaking operation. Journalists soon were describing it as a poorly disciplined force that contained more than its share of thugs posing as soldiers. In a decision that might have been overkill, the Canadian government disbanded the Airborne Regiment. An official inquiry was launched, with the Department of National Defence and the military leadership locked into its sights. Heads rolled, including that of the country's top soldier, Chief of Defence Staff General Jean Boyle.

The Americans faced their own disaster. In October 1993 eighteen soldiers were killed when their helicopter was shot down (Dorn 2005). The reaction of the United States was quick and dramatic: all of its troops were withdrawn from Somalia. With that decision, the UN mission collapsed, which from a Canadian point of view was probably the only good news to come out of Somalia. Certainly the reputation of its military had sunk to a new low.

The Somalia adventure raises a lot of questions. Was it ever genuinely conceived as a humanitarian mission based on peacemaking? If so, how to explain the Canadian decision to select the hyper-aggressive Airborne Regiment for the mission? Was the UN complicit? Recall that the American military was still in a state of euphoria following its predictable triumph a year earlier in Iraq, where, it has often been suggested, it actually was refighting the Vietnam War in order to cleanse a huge blot on its record. Possibly the UN was intimidated by the display of American might and eager to accommodate American-style peacemaking in order not to alienate the one nation on which the peace dividend depended.

Then there is the puzzling decision of the United States to withdraw its troops after the helicopter disaster, rather than redoubling its efforts to impose control over the Somali warlords. Once again, the triumph in Iraq may have been the decisive factor. Probably the last thing the United States wanted was any military engagement that might have blemished its new-found confidence in the invincibility of its troops.

Had the Canadian troops been more disciplined and professional, and the American resolve greater, would the outcome in Somalia have been different? Not necessarily. Somalia has long been of interest to anthropologists (Lewis 1961) because of its bellicose clans, feuds, and warlords. Indeed, it resembles the main source of Taliban insurgents in Afghanistan: the Pashtuns with their history of revolving violence and determined independence (Barth 1959). Somalia, in other words, had all the earmarks of another quagmire for foreign troops.

Was the Somalia intervention doomed from the outset because it was essentially an exercise in imperial policing? Stein and Lang (2007, 301) conclude their insightful study of Canada's military excursion in Afghanistan by questioning whether the time has passed when foreign troops, especially those with a white skin, can barge into a Third World country and expect to be welcomed and triumphant. Somalia may well be a case in point. Incidentally, one can imagine Canada's military leaders in later years lamenting the fact that the one force that was perfectly suited for the Kandahar theatre in Afghanistan no longer was available. I am referring, of course, to the Airborne Regiment.

A final question: does the Somalia case demonstrate that military intervention sometimes can do more harm than good, or is the real lesson the absolute necessity of making certain that a nation's military is a well-oiled machine capable of coping with even the most intractable conflicts? This leads directly to one of the more curious responses to the atrocity-prone Airborne Regiment: David Bercuson's *Significant Incident: Canada's Army, the Airborne, and the Murder in Somalia* (1996).

Bercuson, a full-fledged member of what McKay and Swift have labelled "the new warriors" in Canada, does not deny that the Airborne Regiment had harboured numerous misfits. But the culprit was not the military as an institution. Instead it was the military leadership that had morphed into soldier-managers more concerned with their perks and promotions than fashioning a first-class fighting force. Behind these weak-kneed leaders were the gutless politicians and bureaucrats who ran the country. At a deeper level was the welfare state that had sapped the nation's moral fibre, accounting for the underfunding of the military and the harmful ideology of peacekeeping. Added to this list of misadventures was the 1968 unification of the country's armed forces and the disabling impact of peace on the military following the termination of the Cold War.

Bercuson asserts that only when the Canadian Forces are trained for war rather than peacekeeping will our men and women in uniform be able to serve the country as they should; and only when the welfare state is replaced by one that celebrates the military as its key institution will the rot that has infected the heart and soul of the nation be excised.

Significant Incident is a remarkably clear and engaging early statement about the perspective and goals of the new right in Canada. Just a year after it appeared in print, quite a different study undertaken by a Canadian anthropologist, Donna Winslow, on behalf of the government's formal inquiry into the Somalia case was published. *The Canadian Airborne Regiment in Somalia* (1997) is an ethnographic report based on in-depth interviews and focus groups with former Airborne soldiers and military personnel who were deployed to Somalia, supplemented by documentary research.

Early in her study, Winslow acknowledges the emergence of the soldier-manager role in the military leadership that made Bercuson's blood boil. Winslow explains that the transformation of the Canadian Forces from an institutional to an occupational perspective began in the wake of the Second World War. By "institutional" is meant the traditional image of the military as a war machine. By "occupational" is meant the penetration of civilian culture into the military to the extent that service in it just becomes another job rather than a calling. According to Winslow, changes in the technology of war shifted the focus of officers from managing their troops to managing sophisticated equipment and weapons systems (1997, 24). The upshot was the adoption of conventional administrative and bureaucratic principles, with the accompanying emphasis on promotion, pay, and perks characteristic of civilian life.

The same forces that produced the changes at the top of the military institution affected the troops. The military in the past was justifiably portrayed as a total institution encapsulating every aspect of a soldier's existence. That no longer was completely the case. The unification of the army, navy, and air force into a single entity in 1968 reduced the sense of identity and pride in the branch that one served. Then there was the impact of the Charter of Rights and Freedoms. It compromised the capacity of officers to discipline their troops, condemn behaviour deemed inappropriate such as homosexuality, and maintain standards of fitness and obedience. Then, too, the military's claim to look after soldiers as if they were family took a hit when in the 1970s the practice of making subsidized on-base housing available to military personnel was scrapped. Families and individuals were forced to purchase or rent housing off-base, effectively edging the job closer to a mundane nine-to-five one.

In the context of the shift of the CF from an institutional to an occupational orientation, Canadian Airborne Regiment (CAR) stood out. It stubbornly (one might say ferociously) stuck with the tradition of the heroic warrior and exhibited a degree of in-group solidarity and machoism that largely nullified the impact of the civilian realm.

Members of CAR were derived from the three regiments of the Army: Royal Canadian Regiment (RCR), Princess Patricia's Canadian Light Infantry (PPCLI), and Royal 22^e Regiment (R22^{e}R). CAR recruits were divided into three commandos based on the parent regiment (1 Commando with its ties to Quebec, 2 Commando to the West, and 3 Commando to the Maritimes). By the time that the Somali theatre opened, CAR had moved from Alberta to Camp Petawawa in Ontario.

Membership in CAR was voluntary; those who applied were inclined to crave excitement and were predisposed towards robust action and the thrill of combat. It is well known that the military inculcates a culture of masculinity and sometimes excessive alcoholic consumption, but the members of CAR were over the top. Even before the Somali adventure, problems with discipline were rampant at Petawawa. Fighting was commonplace, and on one occasion an unpopular officer's car was set on fire; the subsequent inquiry went nowhere because of the cloak of silence that enveloped the troops.[2] CAR members considered themselves the elite – real soldiers immune to the rules of military deportment. It seems that even other soldiers recognized CAR members as distinctive – Rambo types intoxicated by the prospect of risky encounters. At the same time they sometimes were regarded as misfits. Indeed, Winslow reveals (1997, 67) that CAR tended to be a dumping ground for the bad apples in other regiments.

The attitude of being special and the bonds of solidarity in CAR were reinforced by the fact that each of the three commandos operated separately and competitively. Another relevant fact was that while there was a regular turnover among officers, the non-commissioned members tended to stay longer, sometimes re-enlisting in the commandos after serving one or more tours of duty. The result was that informal groups crystallized that circumvented the will of the officer class (Winslow 1997, 146).

Gung-ho though the members of the Airborne were, they were quickly disabused of the notion that their tour of duty in Somalia was going to be thrilling and satisfying. First there was the debilitating heat and the constant swirl of dust. Then the harsh conditions of their camp: crude living quarters, shortage of water, inedible food, primitive sanitation causing rampant diarrhoea, and limited communications with loved ones back home. Added to all this was the stress induced by boredom, an inability to distinguish between friend and foe among the Somalis, and an overview of Somali culture before leaving Canada that was ridiculously thin.

If this was not enough to produce anxiety, it seems that the leadership of the camp left a lot to be desired. Not only was the camp poorly organized, but even some of the officers publicly consumed alcohol to excess. Little wonder that the troops attempted to relieve tension with Olympian bouts of booze.

Possibly most depressing of all for the men in uniform was the eventual realization that their humanitarian and security efforts were not appreciated by the Somalis; certainly the welcome mat was not put out for them. It was possibly at this point that some soldiers began to question the Somali mission and redefine Somalis as the enemy.

This brings us to the theft that resulted in the death of Shidane Arone. Despite the stretch of barbed wire around the perimeter of the Canadian compound, apparently it was regularly penetrated by thieves. This was unacceptable to the commandos, and unfortunately for Arone, by the time he was apprehended a handful of them had decided, no doubt pumped up by alcohol, that it was time for drastic action. Apparently the Belgian troops in the UN contingent also treated thieves brutally (Winslow 1997, 243).

Winslow is adamant that the death of Arone cannot be attributed to a few bad apples, especially the main players, Clayton Natchee and Kyle Brown. Instead she attributes the tragic incident to a number of factors (1997, 270): "poor discipline, alcohol consumption, hyper-investment in a rebel warrior identity, a vision of the Somalis as 'the enemy,' environmental and psychological stress, and poor leadership." Equally critical, she adds, was the culture of the Airborne Regiment in which recruits who arrived with a yen for action were socialized to flirt with the extremes.

Although addressing the same topic, the studies of Bercuson and Winslow are quite distinct. Bercuson writes with heat and passion. Winslow is generally satisfied to let the facts speak for themselves. While both studies are first rate, the Winslow volume had a special impact on me. The horror of the deaths of young men in Somalia at the hands of Canada's soldiers notwithstanding, it left me with a sense of sympathy for the star-crossed members of the Airborne Regiment.

The Balkans

We turn now to the complicated and tortuous case of the Balkans, which had a far greater impact on the international community than either Rwanda or Somalia. Yugoslavia, patched together after the Second World War, consisted of six republics, including Bosnia-Herzegovina, Croatia, and Serbia. Under the autocratic leadership of Tito, who successfully carved out a middle position between the two great ideologies of the Cold War, the federation held together. Yugoslavia even became regarded by many Westerners as the one bright spot in the Soviet Union (I spent a few interesting days in Belgrade in 1965).

Then two momentous events intervened. In 1980 Tito died; the country no longer had its indispensable strongman. In 1989 the Berlin Wall was demolished, precipitating the dissolution of the Soviet Union and the end of the Cold War, and creating space for the ethnic rivalries and nationalist aspirations that no doubt had been long simmering under the surface. The consequences for Bosnia, and later for Kosovo, an autonomous province within the Serbian republic, were unspeakable: mass murder, ethnic cleansing, and rape at a feverish pitch rarely matched in history.

The three main ethnic groups in Bosnia before the carnage broke out were the Muslims (or Bosniaks), the Croatians, and the Serbs, the first being the most numerous. Apparently for most of the history of Yugoslavia, relationships among the three groups had been cordial; in fact, intermarriage was not uncommon. Contributing to this happy state of affairs was the largely secular orientation of the population.

By 1992 Bosnia had veered towards a holocaust.[3] The UN swung into action with the UN Protection Force (UNPROFOR), but it was stymied by its inability to impose ceasefires and by the sheer depths of ethnic hatred and violence that engulfed the republic, culminating in the Serbian invasion in 1995. Fully 8000 Bosnian Muslims in Srebrenica were slaughtered, one of the worse cases of mass murder since the Second World War (McKay and Swift 2012, 208).

With the UN force, which included 2500 Canadian troops, rendered impotent (it was a Chapter VI operation), NATO entered the battle zone – the first time that it had engaged in combat since it had been established as a counterweight to the Warsaw Pact in 1949. In the face of massive bombing led by the Americans, the Serbian forces retreated. Soon after, the Dayton Agreement brought the Bosnian war to an end. Three years later in 1998, the focus had switched to Kosovo and its predominantly Muslim population. In response to the massive ethnic cleansing carried out by the Serbs, NATO bombs, with American aircraft in the lead, once again were raining down. The Canadian Airforce participated in the attack, which, unlike Bosnia, had not been authorized by the UN.

By most accounts, the main culprits in the former Yugoslavia were the Serbs. That is plausible, but the Bosniaks and the Croatians contributed their share of carnage. Fulminating the ethnic rivalry and nationalist designs was the religious factor. The Serbs were Orthodox, the Croatians Roman Catholic, and the Bosniaks Muslim. As tensions heated up, secularism was shoved aside by burgeoning religious consciousness and fervour.

This brings us to Samuel Huntington, whose controversial study, *The Clash of Civilizations*, will be featured in chapter 5. In Huntington's words ([1996] 2003, 288), "The war in Bosnia was a war of civilizations." The fact that each of the three main opponents embraced a different religion reinforced his argument, because he regards religion as one of the two defining features of a civilization (the other is language). One of Huntington's key arguments is not only that each civilization constitutes a kin-group writ large, but also that the various nations that constitute a civilization have a built-in tendency to rally around their kin in a crisis. He goes on to show the support of Muslims everywhere for its Bosnian kin, Christians for Croatia, and the Eastern Orthodox community for Serbia.

The one glaring exception in the former Yugoslavia obviously disturbed Huntington: his own country, America, sided with the Muslim populations in Bosnia and Kosovo. The explanation, Huntington suggests, concerns the desire of America to remain on good terms with its Muslim allies such as Saudi Arabia. Or maybe America was motivated by its natural sympathy for the underdog. Then, too, in the international arena America always tries to identify the good and the bad guys and rally to the side of the former. Even if these explanations amount to more than chauvinistic bluster on the part of Huntington, they do not negate the fundamental conclusion: American support for the Muslims casts considerable doubt on the assertion that Bosnia was a war of civilizations.

Eventually the main participants in the former Yugoslavia moved on. Bosnia realized its dreams by becoming an independent state, and it joined Croatia and Serbia as members of the United Nations. In 2009 Croatia was accepted into NATO. By 2015 Bosnia's membership there still was pending. One main obstacle was Western anxiety over the continuing influence of Serbia on Bosnia, with the former's spiritual pipeline to Russia.

Rwanda, Somalia, and the Balkans, then, all are examples of failed states. The impression given by political and military leaders is that failed states are a relatively recent phenomenon on the world stage. But is this true, and what exactly is a failed state, and who gets to define it as such? Was the United States a failed state because of its Civil War, Britain because of Northern Ireland, and France, Spain, and Canada because of their violent secessionist elements: Corsica, the Basques, and Quebec? Was Iraq a failed state because of its cruel suppression of its Kurdish population, or did it become one only after the U.S. invasion? Was Libya actually a functioning (if odious) state under Gaddafi's dictatorial rule? It seems that a failed state often is defined as one that has neither the power nor the international stature to prevent other states from violating its sovereignty. No doubt "failed state" is sometimes a political weapon wielded against one's ideological rivals, and surely "regime change" is regularly undertaken in pursuit of the aggressor's interests.

What is curious about Yugoslavia is that its relative autonomy from Soviet hegemony and its Western inclinations should have given it a head start on the road to an open and viable society when the Cold War ended. It would appear that Yugoslavia is a poignant reminder that while power and interests sometimes determine which states are labelled failures, ethnic, nationalist, and religious rivalries on their own can force a nation to its knees.

The lesson derived by many observers, especially those already ill-disposed towards the UN, was that both its resources and its peacekeeping ideology were woefully inadequate and obsolete in a world driven mad by the progeny of identity politics: rabid ethnic rivalry and nationalism fuelled by religious resurgence. Only NATO or American-led coalitions with or without UN sanction had the tools to get the job done. Of course, the UN lacked the tools either because of the indifference of its member states or outright hostility towards its presumed global mandate.

It is tempting to conclude that the Balkans were a blessing in disguise for NATO. With the Cold War ended, the Western alliance was set adrift. Bosnia and Kosovo pumped a fresh supply of oxygen into it and set the stage for its forays far beyond Europe, notably Afghanistan. It also would be surprising if a certain amount of schadenfreude (pleasure derived from someone else's pain) did not surface in some Third World nations as a result of the blatant evidence that ethnic conflict was not their unique curse.

Peacekeeping

In the wake of the turmoil of the 1990s, hopes for the peace dividend and a renewed and powerful UN were dashed. To many Canadians, the Pearson Peacekeeping Centre, with its international ambitions, must have looked more and more like a kindergarten version of foreign policy. And surely a lot of citizens must have been reluctantly brought around to the viewpoint that in a dangerous world it actually did make more sense to prepare for war rather than peace.

It was this atmosphere that encouraged the opponents of peacekeeping in Canada to go on the attack. One contention was that peacekeeping was nothing more than a myth; it never had been part of the country's past; instead our history has been dominated by glorious war. How this argument was squared with the existence of the Canadian Association of Veterans in United Nations Peacekeeping, with its two dozen chapters across the country and its numerous alumni and mortalities, was conveniently ignored.

Another argument was that even if Canadian soldiers had once been active peacekeepers, peacekeeping was now as dead as the dodo. Nobody did it any more. It is true that Canada's involvement in UN operations had begun to decline as early as the mid-1990s, ironically at the same time that the Chrétien government was extolling the virtues of the UN. By 2010 the country had fallen to sixtieth place in the number of troops UN member nations made available for peacekeeping duties.

What is not true, however, is that peacekeeping was dead. In fact, by the middle of the first decade in the twenty-first century, both the number of missions and troops engaged in UN operations overwhelmed anything that had existed during the Cold War. There were thirteen missions from 1956 to 1978, and twenty-nine between 1988 and 1996 (McKay and Swift 2012, 208). In 2006 alone (Staples 2006) there were eighteen missions. Back in 1991 there were 10,801 peacekeepers in the field. By 2006 the headcount had soared to 66,786.

What is striking about the recent missions is the country of origin of the peacekeepers. The vast majority are from Bangladesh, Pakistan, India, Jordan, and Nepal. Peacekeeping seems to have been transformed into the specialty of Third World or developing nations. First World nations like Canada still honoured their financial commitments to the UN, and those nations that now dominate peacekeeping operations probably welcomed the funds that were provided by the UN. Yet something assaults one's nostrils here. Could it be the odour of neocolonialism?

A third criticism also accepts the reality of Canada's participation in UN missions but dismisses them as abject failures. But what about Egypt, the obvious counter-example? The quick retort is that Nasser kicked out the UN peacekeepers in 1967. Yet the 1956 intervention initiated by Pearson diffused a powder keg. Furthermore, a report produced by the Rand Corporation (cited in Staples

2006, 14), a private U.S. think tank, indicated that UN peacekeeping operations actually have been more successful (and a great deal less costly) than ones launched by the American government.

Overlooked too by the critics are the benefits that peacekeeping accrued to Canada. The apparent altruism helped provide the country with a unifying and pleasing identity. Peacekeeping also enabled Canada to punch above its weight. As a middle-range power, it posed little threat to other nations. Its peacekeeping role enhanced its international reputation, especially among developing nations. Although Canada never was part of the non-aligned bloc straddling the superpowers, it was regarded as less partial than more powerful nations and to some degree acted as an intermediary between the United States and the global community.[4] Not least in importance, peacekeeping encouraged a nation inclined towards pacifism to regard its military in a positive light. Of course, little in life is non-political, and this certainly was true of Canada's peacekeeping role. Peacekeeping more often than not advanced Western interests. In a sense, it amounted to fighting the Cold War with the tools of soft power.

Pearson

This is an appropriate place to take a closer look at the life and accomplishments of Lester B. Pearson. His academic training was in history, and before he entered politics he taught that subject at the University of Toronto. His reputation as an extraordinarily gifted statesman, indeed "the father of UN peacekeeping," was carved in stone following his successful efforts to defuse the Suez Canal Crisis. This is a man, immortalized by the Nobel Peace Prize, who has been embraced by generations of Canadians as the embodiment of the lofty values that they wish to project to the world at large.

Yet there is another side to the story. The British-French aggression in Egypt smacked of neocolonialism at a period in history when colonial empires were on the way out. This raised the ire of Commonwealth nations such as India. Perhaps even more damning, it drew the wrath of President Eisenhower and in doing so posed a threat to the unity of NATO. Arguably it was the possible diplomatic clash between the United States and Britain and France that lit a fire under Pearson. The insertion of an international force between the belligerents provided the Europeans with a face-saving escape route.

Less than a decade later, history repeated itself, this time in Cyprus. Both of the opposing factions, Greece and Turkey, were members of NATO. In 1964 Canada's foreign secretary in the Pearson government, Paul Martin Sr, sent a contingent of troops under UN auspices to Cyprus in an effort to prevent a potential bloodbath. A decade later there still were Canadian troops on the island, and even today not all troops have been recalled. This prompted Dorn (2005), a dedicated supporter of UN peacekeeping, to acknowledge that peacekeeping missions sometimes elongate conflicts rather than terminating them. Yet he might easily have added that aggressive military forays don't fare any better, as the cases of Iraq, Afghanistan, and Libya illustrate. What is really significant about Cyprus is that once again the West, and in this case specifically the Pearson government, may have been motivated less by altruism than by self-serving interests in maintaining the cohesion and integrity of NATO.

If these plausible interpretations of the deeper motives of peacekeeping somewhat tarnish Pearson's legacy, they are child's play in comparison to the attack mounted by Yves Engler in his book *The Truth May Hurt: Lester Pearson's Peacemaking* (2012). According to Engler, Pearson never was a peacekeeper. Instead he was a rabid anti-communist who opposed nuclear disarmament, propelled Canada towards American foreign policy, and supported its wars of imperialism. In short, Pearson was a warmonger of the first order.

In a review of Engler's book, Dummitt (2012) partly dismisses the critique as a left-wing rant that fails to acknowledge Pearson's positive contributions to Canada and the world, but he does not object to the anti-communist and Cold Warrior tags. Nor do other writers such as McKay and Swift (2012, 108): "The lingering paradox of Pearson was that Canada's pre-eminent peacekeeper was also one of its most ferocious Cold warriors." They describe

Pearson (110–11) as a man of his times, "a loyal son of the British Empire" who looked down on the natives and questioned the suitability of Jewish immigrants. McQuaig, in turn (2007, 159), observed that Pearson "subscribed to many Cold War attitudes. In the name of preventing the spread of Communism, Pearson condoned and even clearly supported aggressive U.S. military action in Vietnam."

Then there was Pearson's confrontation with James Endicott, the de facto leader of the influential Canadian Peace Congress in the 1940s and 1950s. Both men were raised as Methodists, and their shared interest in peace seemed to create an understanding between them early in their careers. Then, to borrow an expression from one of my teachers, the scrambled eggs hit the fan. Endicott, who had been born in China where his father had been a missionary, became increasingly strident in his attacks on Western society while at the same time extolling the virtues of communism. According to McKay and Swift (2012, 108), newspapers labelled Endicott "Public Enemy Number One" – the Taliban Jack of his times (a reference to the late Jack Layton's suggestion that the West should initiate peace talks with the Taliban in order to produce a political solution to the Afghanistan War). The Cold Warrior side of Pearson erupted. Endicott became his personal public enemy number one.

At this juncture it would not be surprising if Conservative Party loyalists were willing to overlook Pearson's Liberal credentials and claim him as one of their own. Yet the record remains a mixed bag. As McKay and Swift point out (2012, 144), both hardliners and peaceniks can find support for their ideologies in the Suez Canal Crisis. For the former, it was all about removing friction in NATO. For the latter, it was the birth of peacekeeping.

Pearson's own words in his 1955 book, *Democracy in World Politics*, throw considerable light on his political perspective. While he certainly comes across as a firm anti-communist, he argues that issues and challenges facing humankind are not usually right or wrong, or black and white, but instead an indeterminate grey. He underlines his faith in diplomacy and compromise, and cautions that the degree of force applied in international conflicts must be proportional to the threat. Pearson also disparages the true believer when it comes to politics and contends that the most effective recipe for progress in international politics and diplomacy is neither lofty idealism nor hard-headed realism; instead it is a meaningful combination of the two.

To summarize, Pearson was a Cold Warrior rabidly opposed to communism. But he also was a dedicated believer in the promise of the UN and its peacekeeping ambitions. It should not be forgotten that it was Pearson's government that established universal health care, Old Age Security, and Unemployment Insurance, although the fingers of the NDP and its CCF predecessor were all over these monumental initiatives. Pearson himself thus embodied the twin pillars of idealism and realism. In other words, he was both a lamb and a tiger.[5]

chapter three

Warrior Nation

It is not entirely unusual for ideological opponents to explicitly or implicitly embrace the same potent slogan but endow it with polar opposite meanings. Such has been the case with the catchy image of the 1990s, "the decade of darkness." Even before the 1990s the Canadian military was depressed by the short-war thesis. This was the notion that in the nuclear age an outbreak of hostilities between the two superpowers would be terminated quickly either by a political solution or nuclear annihilation. The short-war thesis posed a threat to the military because it implied that maintaining a conventional army no longer made much sense.

The 1990s saw the military struggling to keep its head above water. Starved of funds, the Somalia debacle weighed it down further and provided politicians with an excuse not to toss it a life jacket. But it was the peace dividend and the prospects of a revitalized United Nations that really seemed to demoralize the armed forces, at least in Canada.

Although Canadian troops were renowned as peacekeepers, that was not the image that they wanted to project. First and foremost they were warriors; peacekeeping was only a sideline. The reaction of the Canadian Forces was to launch a robust defence of their interests. It is difficult to think of a single major peace initiative during the 1990s that was not debunked and undermined by the military, including the peace dividend and the Pearson Centre. Indeed, it would be surprising if at least a portion of the military ranks was not buoyed by the persuasive evidence from Rwanda and Bosnia that peacekeeping operations were a farce.

For UN enthusiasts, the 1990s also were a decade of darkness. In their minds, the dividend for peace represented the most promising hope for global amity and nuclear disarmament since the onset of the Cold War. What they had not anticipated were the several small wars that had erupted by the middle of the decade. Nor, perhaps, were they sufficiently aware of the rock-hard opposition of the American Republican Party (and to some extent the Democrats) to a greater role for the UN and to peacemaking in general. For peaceniks, some solace could be derived from the obvious evidence that UN peacekeeping (or peacemaking) operations had increased dramatically by the end of the decade. Yet the writing was already on the wall. Not only had an expanded role for NATO and American military forays crowded the UN off the stage, but even the meaning of peace was tarnished. As McKay and Swift observed (2012, 209), the UN was at times made complicit as "regime change to promote Western interests is undertaken by armed force ... often in the name of peace."

Although by the mid-1990s the Canadian government had begun to withdraw from peacekeeping operations, it remained publicly an avid fan of the UN. The country's military was quite a different matter. The Canadian Forces were no less determined than the Americans to snuff out any ambitions of the UN to play a more prominent international role and promote peacemaking over war-making.

By the end of the 1990s and into the first decade of the twenty-first century, the Canadian military had switched from defence to offence. Two issues tell the tale: America's Ballistic Missile Defence System and the second Iraq War. According to Stein and Lang (2007, 261), both the civil servants in the North Tower and the military elite in the South Tower of the National Defence Headquarters (NDHQ) in Ottawa connived with friends in Washington to apply American pressure on Canada to participate in the Ballistic Missile program and the 2003 invasion of Iraq. The dire warning pouring out of NDHQ was that if Canada did not join the American ventures, enormous damage would be done to their relationship. Well, the Canadian government ignored the recommendations of its own military, and guess what? The warning of unmitigated disaster never materialized. As Stein and Lang (263) observed about the military, "The advice ... was consistently wrong."

The lesson, I suppose, is that Canadians, as the junior partner in the relationship, worry a great deal about what the Americans think. The reverse is rarely true. The Canadian government's decision did not please the Americans, but apparently they just shrugged their shoulders and proceeded with their war plans. After all, what the Americans sought from Canada probably had less to do with the latter's potential military contribution than with legitimacy and loyalty – a signal to the world that America's causes enjoyed international support, including that of its northern neighbour.

It is no mystery why the Canadian military is so eager to line up alongside its American counterpart. The latter is by far the most powerful in the world. Canadians on exchange programs or training exercises south of the border rub shoulders with the military elite, eyeball the latest advances in military technology, and bask in being at the very centre of global power. Not to be overlooked is the spurt that an assignment with the American military can give to one's career back home. In recent years the impression I have had is that the two militaries have become more closely entwined than ever before. This impression is reinforced by McKay and Swift (2012, 269): "Canada's armed forces have become so deeply integrated with the U.S. military establishment that it is quite reasonable to wonder whether they really are this country's own armed forces."

If we take this to imply that no other Canadian institution can rival the military in interaction with its American counterpart, some people may regard that as another reason to show the armed forces a cold shoulder. Yet surely it is understandable to wish to breathe the same air as the cream of the crop, the recognized experts, regardless of the profession. It might not even be out of line to extend a sympathetic ear to the men and women in uniform who favour armed combat over peacekeeping. Imagine how frustrating it would be to spend years training to be an elite hockey player or tennis star, but never move beyond practice to actual competition. And let's not quibble over equipment: a rifle is only a hockey stick in a different kind of arena.

War as Public Relations

The moment when there no longer was any doubt that Canada's military had ditched peacemaking for war-making can be traced to a specific time, place, and person. In 2006 Canadian troops entered the battlefield in Afghanistan's Kandahar region primarily as a result of the persuasive arguments of a remarkably talented soldier. This was General Rick Hillier, who had become chief of defence staff (CDS) a year earlier.

Thanks to the publication of Clausewitz's *On War* ([1832] 2007), one of the two celebrated classics about war – the other is Sun Tzu's *The Art of War* ([1910] 2009) composed by a Chinese military figure probably in the third or fourth century BCE – it is old hat to portray war as politics by other means. But what has surprised me the most about the Canadian scene is the degree to which war can be reduced to a public relations campaign.

Hillier's rise through the ranks of the Canadian army was impressive, and here I shall only touch on some of the highlights. Born and raised in Newfoundland, like Dallaire his first love was the military. After joining the Regular Officer Training Plan in 1973, he attended Memorial University, graduating in 1975 with a bachelor of science. Ten years later he became a squadron leader while serving in Germany with the Royal Canadian Dragoons, a fabled armoured regiment established as long ago as 1883. He also held a leadership position with the UN peacekeeping mission in Bosnia in 1995. By 2003 he became the commander of the Canadian army and in 2004 the commander of NATO's presence in Afghanistan. A year later he was promoted to the position of Canada's top soldier, the chief of defence staff. Along the way he spent time with the U.S. military at Fort Knox, Kentucky; possibly most impressive of all, he served as deputy commander of the U.S. Army's III Corps at Fort Hood, Texas.[1]

For my purposes, it was Hillier's promotion in 1996 to the command of the 2nd Canadian Mechanized Brigade Group at Petawawa that is noteworthy, because it revealed his early interest in and eventual mastery of the art of public relations. When the Red River flood in Manitoba during the spring of 1997 became a major threat to life and property, the Canadian government put out a call to the army. About 8000 troops led by Hillier made the trip from Petawawa to Winnipeg where their training, discipline, and awesome efforts helped thwart a disaster in the making.

No doubt the army did perform wonders, but the occasion was also a PR triumph. In his autobiography, *A Soldier First* (2009), Hillier points to Manitoba as the turning point in the public's connection to the military. Not only did people from all walks of life express their gratitude, but even the media shelved the usual scepticism about the motives of the army and joined in the applause.

Less than a year later one of the worst ice storms in recent memory devastated eastern Ontario, Quebec, and parts of New Brunswick. Once again Hillier sprang into action. On his orders, about 15,000 troops descended on Ottawa and area from Petawawa and pitched in alongside police and firefighters to rescue people and restore electric power and communications. According to Hillier, residents in Ottawa and elsewhere were enormously grateful to the army, as they should have been. What is interesting, however, is that Hillier's own account of the episode (2009, 188–204) implies that there had never been a request from either the government or his superiors in the Canadian Forces for assistance. In other words, he may well have acted on his own. Surely such initiative is altogether admirable, even if it was partly motivated once more by the opportunity for a public relations coup.

Given the decade of darkness, with the reputation of the military at rock bottom, it is understandable why Hillier saw value in PR. One of his complaints about Bosnia, for example, was that Canadian troops were so dispersed that they never got the recognition they deserved from their allies. This brings us back to Kandahar. Before its story can be told, some background political history is necessary. In 2003 Paul Martin Jr finally managed to push Chrétien aside and become prime minister. His time at the top was destined to be both rocky and short. In the 2004 election, the Liberals were reduced to a minority government, partly because Martin could not extricate himself from the sponsorship scandal that had plagued Chrétien.

In 2005 it became Martin's responsibility to appoint a new CDS. Hillier, despite his impressive record of leadership in Canada and several hotspots abroad, was not first in line for the job, but his grasp of the international scene and his ideas about how to transform the military so that it could deal with the emerging challenge of failed states and terrorism made a huge impression on Bill Graham, Martin's minister of national defence. During subsequent meetings between Martin and Hillier, they found a lot of common ground. Martin too was determined to rebuild the military and improve Canada's relationship with the United States. But they ran into a roadblock when the topic turned to Afghanistan.

It is quite remarkable how highly educated and worldly human beings (academics – except myself, of course – included) can allow personal animosities to cloud their judgment and decisions. Because of the grudge that Martin nursed towards Chrétien, he was determined to tack in the opposite direction of his predecessor. This partly explains why he poured funds into the military and why he courted the Americans, neither of which had been high on Chrétien's agenda. It also goes a long way in making sense of his reluctance to get involved in Kandahar.

Chrétien, of course, much to the pleasure of most Canadians, had nixed Canadian military participation in Iraq, but realizing that in the wake of 9/11 he had to do something to support the country's closest neighbour and ally, he gave a green light to the Afghanistan campaign. In late 2001, without the knowledge of the Canadian public, the elite Joint Task Force 2 (JTF2) was deployed alongside American troops in Kandahar. The following year a Canadian battalion was back in Kandahar for a six-month tour. By 2003 NATO had taken over the UN International Security Assistance Force (ISAF) in Kabul, which included about 2000 Canadian troops. Hillier was appointed commander a year later.

Martin's attention was fixated on other trouble spots such as Darfur in Sudan, Haiti, and the Middle East. But it was because Afghanistan already had Chrétien's fingerprints on it that he recoiled at the prospect of getting involved there. Martin, of course, has not been the only politician who has been consumed by animosity towards his predecessor. I well recall the extent to which

Mulroney went to denigrate the policies and initiatives of his predecessor, Pierre Trudeau. But of course the Chrétien-Martin quarrel was a family feud, a microcosm of the irrational depths of rival ethnic hatred in failed states.

As we all know, Hillier was indeed appointed as CDS and did indeed succeed in his ambition to move Canada's troops from the relative safety of Kabul, where ISAF tried to combine armed combat with nation building, to the heavy fighting alongside the Americans in Taliban-infested Kandahar. It took, however, a lot of persuasion from Hillier to shift Martin to his side.

Hillier had no love for peacekeeping, and his past experience in Bosnia and Kabul had turned him off not only the UN but also NATO, which he described as a bloated and divisive bureaucracy destined for the graveyard. His model of military efficiency and philosophy was the American force, which hunted down its enemies with all guns blazing. If Canadian troops were transferred to Kandahar and began to act like real soldiers, Hillier argued, our allies would be impressed, and the Canadian public would rally behind their fighting men and women.

Martin thought that the reaction of the Canadian public would be exactly the opposite, because Kandahar would obviously not be a peacekeeping operation. In addition, Darfur, Haiti, and the Middle East remained high on his wish list. Hillier assured him that the Canadian Forces had sufficient capacity to address these challenges and also take on the Kandahar mission. Of course, that is not how events unfolded. Kandahar exhausted everything the Canadian Forces had to offer.[2]

With Martin's concerns addressed, the stage was set for the move to Kandahar. At the last moment, however, another obstacle surfaced: the Kandahar operation was too costly; it would have to be scrapped or at least watered down. Then vintage Hillier came to the rescue. As Stein and Lang put it (2007, 195): he "refused to take no for an answer." As a compromise, he insisted that the mission was feasible with a reduced financial commitment. When he added that the Canadian presence in the heart of the battle with the Afghan insurgents would translate into oodles of credit with the Americans, Martin was won over.

From start to finish, Hillier presented the Kandahar venture as a PR exercise, which would not only please Canada's allies but also reconnect the Canadian public with its armed forces. Just as the first Iraq War played a big role in refashioning the image of American soldiers as national heroes in the wake of the Vietnam disaster, the Kandahar mission would finally enable the Canadian military to bury the memory of torture in Somalia.

Is that how the future unfolded? Canadians began to realize that their soldiers had been converted from peacekeepers to a fighting force. Evidence of support also was abundant. Most obvious were the yellow ribbon bumper stickers with the message "Support Our Troops," or the more aggressive slogan, "If you don't stand behind our troops, feel free to stand in front of them." The yellow ribbon is an import from the United States, traced back to the American Civil War and reclaimed by supporters of the Vietnam War.

Not to be overlooked was the Highway of Heroes represented by an overhead bridge on the 401 near the Trenton, Ontario, military base. The symbol of heroism reflected a genuine concern for soldiers who paid the ultimate price. War stimulates an emotional response possibly greater than any other human activity except, perhaps, the death of a child. Who would fail to be moved by the violent demise of young men and women? I know that whenever I watch a war movie or read a book about human suffering in war, composure flies out the window.

In this context, it almost seems to be a sacrilege to point out that the Highway of Heroes might also have served as a PR tool to prod Canadians into accepting the new militarized identity of their nation. Even less tasteful is an interpretation of Canada's role in Afghanistan that is so fundamentally despicable that it should only be whispered: Were the valiant young men and women who died in service there – fully 157 of them by the time Canada withdrew its troops in 2011 – sacrificed at least partly on the altar of PR?

In Hillier's three short years as CDS (later I'll comment on whether he retired or was pushed out by the Harper government), the impression he made on the military and the wider society was enormous. According to Stein and Lang (2007, 151), "Hillier's appointment would fundamentally change the philosophy, the strategy, the organization, and the culture of the Canadian Forces. He would become the most important and influential CDS in living memory." In the view of McQuaig (2007, 70), "Hillier was a whole new kind of general – tough, brash, straight-talking, ready to take on any enemy, exuding a kind of warrior bravado rarely seen in a Canadian general." And McKay and Swift (2012, 233) describe Hillier as "Canada's first superstar soldier of the twenty-first century."

So forceful was Hillier's personality, and so successful were his efforts to expand the capacity and clout of the Canadian Forces, that other government departments, notably Foreign Affairs, were sidelined – collateral damage of a man on a mission. Even before the end of 2005, one Defence official in Ottawa, according to Stein and Lang (2007, 160) was moved to remark that the Canadian Forces "now owned this town."

There is some disagreement about whether Hillier bears the credit (or blame) for Canada's move to the dangerous Kandahar region. Bercuson and Granatstein (2011, 21) insist that it was a collective decision, with Hillier's voice only one of several. Hillier himself in his autobiography (2009, 342–3) is coy about the matter, almost giving the impression that he was only a bystander. Yet most knowledgeable commentators such as Martin (2010, 132) and Stein and Lang (207, 151) agree that Kandahar was nobody's baby but Hillier's.

There is a difference between intellectualism and intelligence. Hillier does not come across as an intellectual, with its attendant (ideal) tolerance for criticism, but he certainly is an intelligent man. The importance of this quality in a military leader has been clarified by Clausewitz in his analysis of military genius ([1832] 2007, 44–60). Clausewitz remarks that successful commanders are almost never accomplished scholars, but adds (97), "No great commander was ever a man of limited intellect." He claims that war is the most unpredictable activity undertaken by humans. It always is wrapped in uncertainty, never unfolding according to preconceived military plans. In short, it is a game of chance (46). In this context, I can't help but think about the number of times that Canadian political and military leaders complained that their goals in

Afghanistan were continuously thwarted by unanticipated obstacles such as the porous Pakistan border and the resurgence of the Taliban in Kandahar. Had they forgotten their Clausewitz?

Clausewitz's point is that it requires a leader of high intelligence to cope with the unpredictable nature of war. In addition, a leader must have a good grasp of the relevant political issues as well as an intuitive capacity to know how to adjust to a fluid environment. Admire Hillier or not, it strikes me that in terms of Clausewitz's portrait of military genius, he is the perfect commander. Higher praise there cannot be.

Influence, Manipulation, and Force

When the Conservative Party took over in 2006, it was the recipient of a splendid gift from the chastened Liberals: the war in Afghanistan, especially the violent Kandahar mission. The manner in which the Conservatives used the war to advance their right-wing agenda and used the nation's institutions to promote the military constitutes an intriguing case study of power. Like any phenomenon that comes under the scrutiny of academics, power has been rendered complex, a menu of proliferating concepts. Three of the main ones are influence, manipulation, and force. Influence, with its aim of manufacturing consent, looks like soft power, while force connotes hard power. Both influence and force are usually overt. In contrast, manipulation is covert; it involves tinkering with people's lives without their awareness, with the added wrinkle that the outcome is normally contrary to their interests.

Of course these are abstract concepts. In real life the behaviour that each of them purports to represent is all jumbled together. Although in any specific setting one of the concepts may appear to be the best fit, often this is more a matter of judgment and guesswork than logic on the part of the observer. With these cautionary remarks, I turn now to some examples of manipulation. High on the list is the Senate scandal involving a secret $90,000 payment to Mike Duffy by Nigel Wright, Harper's chief of staff at the time. Then there was the robocall scandal during the 2011 election, which involved tricking voters into believing that their polling stations had changed. Dirty tricks at the 2007 summit at Montebello and the 2010 summit in Toronto, including agents provocateurs and fake laws, speak volumes about manipulation.

One example of force concerns the Message Event Proposal that prevented Harper's caucus and civil servants from communicating in public without first obtaining a green light from the Prime Minister's Office (PMO). This was not a case of influence, because its targets had no choice but to obey. Nor was it deception, because it was instituted openly. Other examples are the two times the Conservative government prorogued Parliament, threats to defund charitable organizations such as Oxfam that did not conform to Conservative ideology, and firing individuals, or making their lives so miserable that they resign, who refused to knuckle under the government's ideology.[3]

It should be pointed out that quite a number of the Conservative Party's manoeuvres appeared to be hybrids straddling persuasion and manipulation. Consider, for example, the over-the-top celebration of the 1812 War with the United States. On the surface this was merely a harmless romantic footnote to the nation's past, a persuasive reminder to take our history seriously, but underneath it conveyed the message that our past has been forged in war. An even more blatant example concerns the guides made available to prospective new Canadians (see McKay and Swift 2012, 15). In the 2005 version predating the Harper regime, *A Look at Canada*, military images are nowhere to be found. In the 2009 version, *Discovering Canada*, fully twenty of thirty images in the history section evoke the military. The unspoken message is that Canada is no exception to the storyline that the history of a nation is the history of war.

Reinventing history is the appropriate label for these political manoeuvres, and as Hobsbawm (1983, 4) has pointed out, it is a normal phenomenon as societies attempt to reconcile the past with the social changes of the present. According to Kuhn (1962), it even happens in science; periodically new textbooks are written to present a picture of steady, cumulative knowledge rather than the abrupt paradigmatic shifts that are closer to reality. If there has been anything different about the Conservative approach, it has been the reversal of the causal arrows. Normally it is the past that has to be tinkered with so that it is rendered compatible with the present. For the Conservatives, the present is the dependent variable. It is the weight of the past that gives it shape.

War and Sports

Three themes will guide this section: first, the manipulation of sports, especially hockey and football, to promote militarism; second, sports as an alternative to war; third, sports as a reinforcer of war.

The linkage between war and sports has a long history in America, but it was not until 2006 that a similar connection became apparent in Canada. That was the year that the Grey Cup was turned into a military spectacle. McKay and Swift (2012, 251) capture the scene beautifully: soldiers escorting the players from the airport, parachutists showing their stuff, tanks, heavy artillery, the boom of shells after a touchdown, and the inevitable recruiting tents. Commenting on the 2011 Grey Cup, Lawrence Martin wrote (2011), "Chalk up another public relations triumph for the governing Conservatives. They turned the opening ceremonies of our annual sports classic into a military glorification exercise."

Soon Forces Appreciation Nights became an annual Blue Jays event, with the players decked out in camouflage uniforms. But not surprising, it was hockey that became the focus in Canada for the sports-war duet. The Memorial Cup was donated by the Ontario Hockey Association in 1919 in remembrance of Canadian soldiers who lost their lives in the First World War, a most laudable and deserved gesture, in my opinion, even if that ghastly war amounted to a contest between imperial rivals rather than the pursuit of freedom and democracy. But by 2014, with London as the host city, the emblem of Junior A hockey supremacy too had become a military spectacle. The cup arrived in the city by a Canadian Forces helicopter and was escorted for a ceremony at the cenotaph by an armoured motorcade.

Individual soldiers or their families, including on one occasion my own relatives, were singled out during NHL games to the applause of the spectators. The Stanley Cup was carted off to Afghanistan, and entertainers such as Rick Mercer, and especially hockey icons such as Guy Lafleur, mingled with the troops. There is, of course, every reason to put a little joy into the daily routine of soldiers risking their lives far from home. Yet one wonders how many of them thought about the possibility that both the game of hockey and the military were being manipulated to serve political ends.

Then there is Don Cherry. In his *Hockey Night in Canada* broadcasts, he never tires of extolling the virtues of the nation's fighting men and women and unquestioningly supporting the country's military adventures. Little wonder that the Royal Military College presented him with an honorary degree.

Hockey certainly has proved useful in the effort to remake Canada into a warrior nation, but it is not the sport that most closely resembles war. That honour belongs to football. Consider this passage by John McMurtry (1971), a philosopher who in his youth was a linebacker with the Calgary Stampeders: "The family resemblance between football and war is, indeed, striking. Their languages are similar: 'field generals,' 'long bomb,' 'blitz,' 'take a shot,' 'front line,' 'pursuit,' 'good hit,' 'the draft' and so on. Their principles and practices are alike: mass hysteria, the art of intimidation, absolute command and total obedience, territorial aggression, censorship, inflated insignia and propaganda, blackboard manoeuvres and strategies, drills, uniforms, formation, marching bands and training camps. And the virtues they celebrate are almost identical: hyper-aggressiveness, coolness under fire and suicidal bravery." Nothing more needs to be said.

Eventually the intrusion of the military into the arenas and playing fields of the nation spawned a robust critical response. Lawrence Martin (2012) pointed out that although the Conservatives are supposedly all for less government, in reality they have pushed politics into virtually every corner of society, including the realm of sports. Another journalist, Cathal Kelly (2014), revealed his disgust with the camouflage-clad Blue Jays in his typical punchy prose.

Not to be overlooked was the appearance of an online forum called "Left Hook," the brainchild of a political scientist, Tyler Shipley. In 2013 he accused the government and the compliant media and sports executives of subverting sports in order to promote political ends, namely the imperialist Afghan mission. Shipley lamented the passing of the days when fans could attend a sports event without being bombarded with military jingoism.

Sports without War is an organization with goals identical to Left Hook. In one of its blogs, a writer identified only as Laura K (2013) observes that when war and sports are fused, spectators of sports become spectators of war, and war becomes just another sport. In 2014 "Sports without War" pulled off a public relations coup at the expense of the Toronto Maple Leafs (see Shipley 2014). It created a press release pretending to be crafted by the Leafs' organization and announcing that the next Military Appreciation Night would feature a moment of silence for Afghan civilians who had become "collateral damage" in the war against terrorism. Furthermore, their families residing in Canada would be provided free admission. Ouch!

The second and third themes – sports as an alternative to war and as a reinforcer of war – open with the perspectives of two of the most renowned figures in modern history: Nelson Mandela and George Orwell. Mandela believed that sports had the capacity to inspire people to coexist in harmony. Nowhere was this more apparent than in connection to the South African national rugby team, with its reputation as a bastion of white supremacy, players and fans alike. When Mandela pushed that history aside and embraced the team during the run-up to the 1995 Rugby World Cup hosted by South Africa, his fellow countrymen, regardless of class and colour, sat up and took notice, as did a lot of people in the international community.

Orwell approached sports from the polar opposite direction. One of his most memorable quips (1945) was that sport "is war without the shooting." He especially detested the degree to which nationalism is enflamed by sport and described contests between national teams as "mimic warfare."

Throughout my life I have shared Mandela's view that sports unite people and sublimate aggression that may engender conflict, even war. On a motorcycle trip to Timbuctu in West Africa during my youth, I joined a pick-up basketball game in Mali and a soccer game in Burkina Faso. On both occasions barriers of national origin fell to the wayside. I might add that whenever I watch a game, either in person or on the TV screen, the moment that thrills me more than any other is when the combatants come together at the end of the contest with their hands stretched out in a gesture of sportsmanship and respect.

Support for Mandela's perspective is reflected in the impact of the U.S. table tennis team's invitation to China in 1971. It led to a diplomatic thaw, culminating in Richard Nixon's triumphant visit a year later. Yet the evidence for Orwell's perspective is much more abundant. In the 1936 Olympics in Germany, Joe Lewis was defeated by Max Schmeling, who was embraced by the Nazi Party as a heroic symbol of Aryan superiority (in a rematch in New York City, Lewis exacted his revenge). At those same Olympic games, Jesse Owens won four gold medals – a slap in the face to Hitler, who apparently shunned the American idol.

Athletes rarely step out of line and oppose the ideology and power structure of their countries. Possibly the most famous example was Muhammed Ali. He became a symbol of the opposition to the Vietnam War when he refused to be drafted into the army. At the 1968 Olympics, two American athletes, Tommy Smith and John Carlos, gave the Black power salute during the presentation of their medals, a very public gesture against the racism embedded in their country. Examples in Canada are much thinner. Blue Jays star Carlos Delgado famously signalled his opposition to the invasion of Iraq by remaining seated during the playing of "God Bless America"; a similar anti-war gesture was made by basketball whiz Steve Nash.

Because sports are so closely identified with a nation's central values and power structure, athletes who don't toe the line risk being ostracized by both their teammates and their fans. Much more acceptable than the protests by Delgado and Nash was Wayne Gretsky's gushing support for Harper shortly before the

2015 election. Although the impact of his gesture on the country was ambiguous, one thing was crystal clear: his famous timing on that occasion had deserted him.

Owners and executives of sports teams, as well as league officials, contend that sports and politics should not be mixed. Yet if that is the case, how do we interpret the intrusion of the military into hockey, baseball, and football? Obviously sports and politics do mix, but it is considered legitimate only when the reigning ideology is reinforced.

If further evidence of nationalism stirred up by international sports is needed, ponder the bitter outcome of a three-game soccer series in 1969 between El Salvador and Honduras. Such was the mayhem both on the field and in the stands that the two countries terminated diplomatic relations, and it was not until 1980 that a peace treaty was signed. But we don't have to go that far away for similar evidence. The magnificent 1972 hockey series between Canada and the Soviet Union was political from start to finish: the West against the East, capitalism versus communism. Who can forget Paul Henderson's heroics, or his spontaneous declaration that the Canadian team had just chalked up a victory for capitalism?

More than a quarter century ago, Hargreaves (1982, 121) asserted that sports have become the new opiate of the people. When I explained his argument during a graduate seminar, my female students strongly disagreed; sports might be a drug of preference for their male peers, they allowed, but not for women. Throughout history sports have been used to form male character conducive to war activity. It was in this context that the Duke of Wellington quipped that Waterloo was won on the playing fields of Eton. Reinforcing this theme are the insights of Mangan (2006): both the playing field and the battleground are sites of legitimate aggression; the image of masculinity forged in the one is replicated in the other. Little wonder that sports fans, especially men, appear to be receptive to the military carnival in the arenas and playing fields of the nation.[4]

To conclude, what is surprising about the manipulation of sports to foster a war ethos is that it took so long to take root in Canada.

It is difficult to know whether credit should be given to Hillier or Harper. Presumably on this matter they saw eye to eye. Sports were the perfect medium for Hillier's slogan, "Recruit the Nation." As for Harper, he was reputed to be a dedicated hockey fan and even published his own book (2013) on the game. It did not require a huge leap in imagination on his part to appreciate the payoff for his vision of a militarized Canada if he hitched a ride on the nation's chariot to sports heaven.

The link between sports and war sometimes takes a curious turn. Apparently Stephen Crane, the author of the American classic *The Red Badge of Courage* (1895), had no first-hand experience with war; his inspiration was drawn partly from his study of manly sports. Then there was the occasion in Nigeria during the Vietnam War when a U.S. Peace Corps volunteer remarked to me that the evening news reports back home on the daily body count bore an eerie resemblance to the accompanying summary of the sports scores.

Even the classical studies of Sun Tzu and Clausewitz have some relevance to the link between war and sport. Sun Tzu's *The Art of War* has had an influence on the business world and the sports world, possibly because of the emphasis that he places on deception ([1910] 2009, 3). Then there is Clausewitz's assertion that defence is more important and effective than offence. One only has to recall the stunning success of the Montreal Canadiens and the Edmonton Oilers in their heydays. Certainly both teams were loaded with scoring geniuses, but they also were blessed with gifted defence-men and goalies. Compare the recent Oilers team to the Gretzsky and Beliveau eras: a powerhouse up front, and sad sacks at the rear. Even mediocre teams can scratch out victories via clever defence, and when it's playoff time little else is heard except the virtue of defence.

Bercuson (1996, 30), incidentally, takes exception to the comparison of war to any other realm such as business and sports, his point being that war is unique. On this issue he is in good company. Clausewitz ([1832] 2007, 144) has made exactly the same point: "War is a special activity, different and separate from any other pursued by man."

Why the Switch from Peacekeepers to Warriors?

9/11

The terrorist attack on America prompted sympathy from all around the world and probably more than anything accounts for the rapid expansion of Canada's military. There was a great deal of understanding for America's aggression against the Taliban in Afghanistan and the hunt for bin Laden. However, it is commonplace now to suggest that this may have been precisely the reaction that bin Laden hoped for. Possibly he had borrowed a page from the playbook of the far left about the benefit of exposing the contradictions in American society and deepening those with its enemies. Just as the Soviet Union was brought to its knees partly as a result of the invasion of Afghanistan in the 1990s, a similar fate might be visited on America. Curiously, it was this same risk that cautioned President Obama during his second term in office to limit military intervention in ISIL-held territory.

Such is the complexity of life, with its range of personal interests, that it is rare if somebody doesn't benefit from calamity. From the perspective of Western militaries, deprived of their Cold War opponent, there must have been a conflicted sense of relief that a new and dangerous enemy had crawled out from under the rocks. This provided an opportunity for George W. Bush and his allies not only to roll out the war machine but also to aim its arsenal beyond the confines of Afghanistan. Obviously I have Iraq in mind, the regrettable adventure that did much to erode the sympathy of the international community. Of course, critics abroad probably would have been more understanding of America's scattergun approach had it been their country that bin Laden targeted.

New Forms of Conflict

The 1990s were fragmented by fanatic ethnic rivalry and nationalism, reflecting a shift from interstate to intrastate conflict. Behind these changes were the end of the Cold War and globalization. The first removed the lid from a potent mixture of hatred and ambition that had long been brewing. The second also played a role, because globalization generates not only similarity everywhere but also new expressions of heterogeneity, such as the explosion of small nationalisms. The argument has been that the United Nations lacks the capacity, and maybe the stomach, to cope with these complex and dangerous types of conflict. Thus the green light for Western military intervention.

All this seems to make sense, but an irksome question arises: When Western forces attacked Afghanistan, Iraq, and Libya and attempted to influence the internal affairs of Ukraine and Syria, were intrastate conflicts not transformed into interstate ones? Moreover, was burgeoning global terrorism not by definition an interstate phenomenon? Incidentally, Scott Taylor (2014) contends that the West committed a major blunder by going after Saddam Hussein, Muammar Gaddafi, and Bashar Assad. As Taylor points out, all three Arab leaders were secularists opposed to the Muslim fanatics of the Al-Qaeda variety.

Sudan, Rwanda, and Balkans

Nothing more needs to be added about these prime examples of intrastate conflict, but they warrant being highlighted here because of the impact they had on Canada's military and political establishments.

Sharp Increase in UN Peace Operations

There was a time when Canada was celebrated as the leading contributor to UN peacekeeping, largely because of the limited number of missions and participating nations. This all began to unravel by the 1990s in face of the sharp increase in missions and nations willing to provide the necessary troops. Discovering that it could no longer compete in the growth industry of UN peacekeeping, but eager to sustain its high profile, Canada shifted its support to the more aggressive version of peacekeeping associated with NATO and American foreign policy.

Cultural Identity

The same dynamic that lies behind intrastate conflict and failed states also partly accounts for Canada's drift towards its Western allies. According to Huntington ([1996] 2003), wars are no longer fought for economic or territorial gain, but rather as an expression of cultural (or civilizational) identity. Nobody would be less surprised than Huntington that Canada largely abandoned its internationalism and rallied around its cultural kin.

With the election of Harper's government, Canada turned its back on the UN. The world must have taken note, because in 2010 for the first time Canada failed in its quest for a rotating seat on the Security Council. Canadians, possibly the majority, were not pleased. Yet they might have been less critical of Harper and his government had they appreciated the magnet of cultural identity in recasting one's allegiance behind its civilizational kindred. That is, if they didn't discard Huntington's thesis as narrow-minded nonsense.

Unlike Canada, America has a long history of being anti-UN, and why not? America is an empire. It fully expects to have its way internationally and resents a rival body that dares to challenge its domination. When the UN was established in 1945, it consisted of 51 member states. Now there are more than 190, all of which have a vote in the General Assembly, some of which bristle at U.S. influence and affluence. In many respects America is a rather benign empire, generous in its support for people snared in natural disasters abroad and perfectly willing to export its brand of democracy.

Influence of Elites

Although political and military leaders such as Martin, Harper, and Hillier obviously were central figures in Canada's turn towards militarism, academic elites who shared Harper's vision of a right-wing utopia steeped in military glory were not idle. Nor were they inconspicuous. The reason is that conservative commentators have greater access to the media nowadays than do their ideological rivals.

Two of Canada's most prominent public intellectuals are David Bercuson and Jack Granatstein. Bercuson's book on the torture in Somalia, it will be recalled, laments the crippling impact of socialism on the country and portrays a robust military as indispensable for healing the nation. Whether or not we agree with his views, one thing cannot be denied: the man can write. *Significant Incident* is a paragon of academic prose.

In their joint evaluation of the Afghanistan adventure, Bercuson and Granatstein labelled it a just war. More surprising is their portrayal of Canada's military presence there to some extent as a PR exercise. For example, they comment (2011, 22) that Canadian troops were in Afghanistan to impress America and other allies and to show that Canada did more than peacekeeping and no longer was a free rider. I would have thought that these accomplished scholars were too sophisticated to express these views openly, even if they believed them to be true.

Granatstein, who did his undergraduate studies at the Royal Military College, has no love for peacekeeping. He once observed (see McKay and Swift 2012, 186), quite plausibly in my opinion, that peacekeeping in the Canadian psyche often amounts to anti-Americanism. When he was appointed director and CEO of the Canadian War Museum in 1998, he was aghast to discover that the entire third floor was devoted to Canada's participation in UN peacekeeping missions. He quickly had that "junk" (my word) replaced with the archaeological evidence of a past steeped in military adventure. Curiously, this small drama unfolded during Chrétien's rule. The fact that nobody in the PMO prevented Granatstein's dramatic reaction may reveal the extent to which peacekeeping was already fading into the shadows.

A Harper fan, at least as far as war is concerned, Granatstein has commented that no other government in the past half-century has served the military better. Granatstein regretted that Canada's love affair with the UN and peacekeeping was expressed in the unwillingness to join George W. Bush's invasion of Iraq – another just war in the academic's opinion. Granatstein has stated that he fully believed that Saddam Hussein possessed weapons of mass destruction. All that I can hope is that readers don't jump to the conclusion that our noted scholar's ideological lenses were so opaque that he was unable to see what was obvious to much of the world community.[5]

Demography

Usually when the age profile of a country is scrutinized for its impact on society, such as explosive race relations and counterculture tendencies, the focus settles on young people, especially males. Yet, as a perceptive journalist, Michael Valpy, has pointed out (2012), senior citizens of both sexes can have their own unique impact on a society. As the baby boomers have aged they have grown more conservative and security-conscious, precisely the ingredients conducive to rallying around a more militarized nation.

NAFTA

As Melnyk observes (2011), the 1988 Free Trade Agreement initiated by Mulroney's Progressive Conservative Party opened the door for possible closer political and ideological bonds with America. In this situation, it was only a matter of time before the military joined the parade. Indeed, in late 2015 I began to hear rumours of the possible formal union of the Canadian and American forces. There also were plans to establish up to seven Canadian military bases around the globe. If that isn't suggestive of an integrated political and military ideology, I don't know what would be. Harper loyalists, I suppose, can only hope that Justin Trudeau has enough common sense and fortitude to do the right thing for Canada's international clout and reputation.

Canada as a Free Rider

I once listened to a neighbour who seemed almost to be on the verge of a fit as she ripped into her adopted country, Canada (she was born and raised in the United States), for its hypocritical support of UN peacekeeping. In her view, Canada was a pathetic free rider; UN peacekeeping was only a ruse to avoid the financial commitment that a responsible member of the Western hemisphere should shoulder. But finances may be exactly the point. Consider Boutros-Ghali's 1992 vision for the world: "Peace-keeping operations approved at present are estimated to cost close to $3 billion in the current 12-month period ... Against this, global defence expenditures at the end of the last decade had approached $1 trillion a year, or $2 million per minute."

In the interest of public order, and as a kindness to right-wing enthusiasts, who are noted for their fiscal discipline, this message should not be exposed to them en masse; otherwise there might be a stampede to sign up with the local UN chapter.

Aspirations of Military

It is, of course, superfluous to point out that the military establishment had a vested interest in its expansion and warrior stature. But had it preferred the status quo, the previous factors would not have found the soil so fertile. This is why the dreams of the military must be added to the list.

Winners and Losers

Who wins as a result of the switch from peacekeepers to warriors? First of all, the military itself. Second, the armaments industry. Third, anyone who would prefer Canada to be more like America. Fourth, individuals who have attached themselves to the military's rising fortunes such as the athletes and media stars featured earlier. Fifth, people to the right of the political spectrum. Sixth, the affluent, regardless of political affiliation, because the military exists as a reserve force when social protest gets out of hand.

What is lost? First, the image of Canada at home and abroad as an unobtrusive, fair, and peaceful nation. Second, Canada's support for the UN, especially peacekeeping operations. Third, the country's former reputation of having a foreign policy quasi-independent of the United States. Fourth, diplomacy and compromise – collateral damage of the swing towards military solutions. Fifth, reduced or at least unchanging economic prospects for the poor, unless we ignore the military's reserve force status and accept the Conservative line that poverty is a product of the welfare state.[6] Sixth, freedom. Paradoxically, the Conservative Party's relentless attack on big government is motivated by the desire to provide citizens with more freedom, but that goal is sometimes compromised or even negated. One reason is that any government has to contend with the fact that not all values can coexist. A choice often must be made between them. For example, the Harper government's celebration of the individual could not be absolute, given the threat that child molesters and sexual deviants posed for family values. Then, too, just as small government relaxes its grip on the individual's economic performance, more prisons are built, more police hired, and the military expanded. In other words, the Conservative agenda simultaneously generates greater freedom for the individual while ramping up the state's apparatus of heavy-handed control. Curiously, this bears an uncanny resemblance to the apparent contrast between the economic and political realms in post-war Vietnam. On a recent visit there, I was struck by the individualistic, dog-eat-dog character of the former and the dictatorial character of the latter.

Some Reflections

Had Martin remained prime minister after 2005, would it have made any difference regarding the Afghanistan mission? Probably not much. He already had agreed to shift Canadian troops to Kandahar, and as mission creep sets in, plus the rationalization common to wars that the fight must go on so that fallen soldiers did not die in vain, not to mention the apparently vague exit plans, Canada's newly fashioned fighting force was caught in a web partly of its own making. It is possible, however, that Martin would have balked at the extension of the mission from 2007 to 2009 and then to 2011, and probable that he would not have interpreted the war as an opportunity to undermine Parliament and whip the citizenry into line.

Had Chrétien served another term as prime minister, would the Afghanistan mission have turned out differently? Quite possibly. He likely would have finessed the situation so that Canada's commitment was minimal, certainly avoiding the Kandahar theatre; and it is doubtful that he would have appointed gung-ho Hillier as CDS. Chrétien was not as complex a character as Pearson, with the latter's propensity for promoting peace while blazing away at communism, but he sure was a wily politician. If Pearson was both a lamb and a tiger, Chrétien was a fox.

Usually it is assumed that the military has a better fit with the Conservatives than with the Liberals, but Hillier's relationship with Harper was much more brittle than it had been with Martin. As Joe Clark (2013, 97) has commented about the former Conservative leader, "This is a notoriously controlling prime minister." Harper was not charmed by Hillier's independence and high profile. In contrast, Martin and Hillier seemed to hit it off from the outset, possibly because Martin admired Hillier's decisiveness and maybe simply because the Liberal leader was a more confident individual than his successor.[7]

There is another reason Harper may have soured on Hillier: his possible intrusion into the realm of policy. If that were so, it helps to explain Wells's otherwise baffling assertion (2013, 408) that the Harper administration may actually have strengthened the nation's democratic credentials. In my judgment, this charge is baseless. Hillier certainly was a forceful leader, even at times giving the impression of being a borderline dictator. However, that probably just reflects the hierarchy and discipline characteristic of the military institution. Of course, there were occasions when Hillier seemed to exceed his authority, such as his decision to sign the agreement with the Afghanistan government about the handling of Taliban prisoners. Yet I can only think of a single example – the Kandahar mission – where he attempted to manoeuvre the political dimension of war in a specific direction, and even there the clear understanding was that the politicians were in charge, otherwise he would not have had to expend so much effort trying to persuade them. Indeed, the glaring case when military intrusion did transpire occurred before he became CDS: the efforts of the armed forces establishment to push the Canadian government to support America's plans for the ballistic missile program and the Iraq War.

If I have any criticism about Hillier in this context, it is that he was altogether too compliant about the nation's war ambitions, at least in public. In this respect, he was only following the model set out by Clausewitz. The famous German military theorist ([1832] 2007, 252–6) left no room for ambiguity regarding the relationship between politicians and soldiers. The latter must always be subordinate to the former. Soldiers, Clausewitz contends, are wrong to complain about political influences on the conduct of war, because the latter is a political phenomenon from start to finish. He does add that just as military commanders must have a grasp of the broader political situation, politicians, if war is to be successful, must possess an understanding of military issues.

Do circumstances account for the prominence and success of Hillier and Harper, or is it necessary to resort to the Great Man thesis? Hillier's reputation is that of a charismatic leader, but what does that tell us? Charisma more often than not is an attribute attached to a leader after the fact. Indeed, it is another example of reinventing history. When so-called charismatic leaders are examined in depth, usually it surfaces that there was a great deal of turmoil among competitors for the top job. It is only when one of them rises above the others that he or she is adorned with extraordinary personal qualities.

In Hillier's case, circumstances were propitious for a strong leader, notably the impact of 9/11 and the impetus to move beyond the decade of darkness. Nevertheless, room in one's analysis always must be made for an individual's personal qualities. Hillier was (and presumably remains) an extraordinarily capable human being. He breathed new life into his beloved military, and who can blame him for fertilizing his own garden? What if he had been the minister of health? Or what if there were a federal Ministry of Education, with Hillier at the helm? We would all have been enthralled by his determined and innovative leadership. Of course, this raises the question as to whether a potent military is as important for society as health and education.

Hillier possesses another attribute that is worth considering: optimism.[8] In his autobiography, he refers to optimism as a "force multiplier," which are the same words that Harari chose (2002, 215) to capture the essence of the leadership of an American icon, Colin Powell. Optimism and charisma do not always coincide. Reagan had both, while Pierre Trudeau (and possibly Diefenbaker) was charismatic but not obviously optimistic.[9] Chrétien was an optimist but lacked charisma, much like Karl Marx, who was so certain that socialism and then communism would obliterate capitalism that he worried that he would not manage to complete his great work, *Capital*, before the revolution had erupted.

This brings us back to Harper. He certainly was not a charismatic leader, nor was he an optimist. He ruled with the constant concern that the deep roots of liberalism in the Canadian psyche would resurface and thwart his ambition to convert the country into a conservative bastion before he was forced out of office. This goes a long way to explain his almost ruthless control of his caucus, and his assaults on the nation's democratic traditions, especially Parliament.

Was Harper, then, a fascist? This is the accusation levelled by some commentators such as Bourrie (2015, 340), while former Parliamentary budget officer Kevin Page has referred to Harper as "Putinesque" (see Barlow 2015, 7). In this context, it often was claimed that Harper had a hidden agenda, which strikes me as nonsense. Before he became prime minister, his vision for the nation was set out in crystal clear terms in his famous Civitas speech (Harper 2003). There he distinguished between economic and moral conservatism. The first type, he argued, had triumphed long ago; even his political rivals had embraced fiscal conservatism. The real battle, he thought, concerns moral conservatism, which amounts to destroying every vestige of the just society with its welfare frills and replacing it with the values of conservatism: individual liberty and responsibility, merit rather than handouts, and the hallowed family.

What about Harper's incrementalism? This was the strategy of achieving change inch by inch, so slowly that people don't even realize when a foot has been gained, then a yard. Yet this strategy was described in the media with sufficient regularity that to characterize it as hidden is rather silly.

It may be more accurate to describe Harper as an especially enamoured neoliberal rather than a fascist. Neoliberalism promotes the individual over the group and favours private ownership and an unfettered open market. It would be just as misleading to label him a neo-fascist. The difference between a neo-fascist and a right-wing conservative pivots on their attitude towards Jews. For the neo-fascist, Jews are the children of the Devil, the polluters of civilization. For right-wing conservatives, at least those who are born-again Christians, Jews are God's chosen people. This brings us to Harper's strong support for Israel. Anti-Semitism often has been traced to the charge that Jews killed Christ. Yet anti-Semitism predated Christianity and has persisted long since biblical times. It might be thought that it has been Harper's revulsion about the Holocaust that has led him to Israel's side. That may have been a factor, but it probably was less important than his religious orientation. Although raised in the United Church, when he took up residence in Calgary he converted to the fundamentalist movement. Later in Ottawa he joined a small working-class evangelical church (McDonald 2010, 19–23), a fact that inexplicably escaped the knowledge of the media. One central tenet of evangelical Christianity is that Christ is destined to return to earth – not just any old place, but Israel. Jews in Israel, then, are the guardians of a saviour who is not their own.

Although Israel has been criticized from many quarters for using excessive force to quell Palestinian uprisings and destroy the military capacity of its foes in the Middle East, Harper has not been one of them.[10] Possibly he agrees with Dershowitz (2003), who has asserted that if Israel ever loses a single war, the nation will cease to exist. Or maybe Israeli aggression has a different source altogether. When its Western allies attacked Iraq, Afghanistan, and Libya, they did not waste time worrying about unleashing disproportionate force. With that model as a guide, why should Israel behave otherwise?

Both Harper and Hillier were highly disciplined leaders, but that is just about all that they had in common. One main difference was that Hillier, raised in the Salvation Army faith, has stated (2009, 24) that he is "not a particularly spiritual guy." Another difference is that Hillier was essentially a one-issue man. All his attention and effort was directed to rebuilding the military; politics seemed for him to be an unavoidable distraction. A single issue also dominated Harper – the quest for a conservative make-over of the country.[11] But more so than for Hillier, a secondary focus riveted his attention: the military and its potential to catapult the political ball into conservative heaven.

What disturbed many people about Harper, possibly even some of his party faithful, was the impression that almost any means was justified in pursuit of his political ends. One example was the two times that he prorogued Parliament, first in order to avoid a motion of confidence engineered by the conspiring opposition parties, and second to cool down parliamentary critics in the midst of the scandal about the ill treatment of insurgent prisoners handed over by the Canadian troops to Afghan civilian control (Smith 2013).

This latter manoeuvre is almost benign compared to Harper's eventual treatment of military veterans, especially those who returned with damaged bodies and minds. At the outset of Harper's rule, he praised the military at every opportunity. A few years later he had shut down Veterans Affairs offices, reduced the benefits for combat men and women, and – hard to believe – even went to court to argue that the Canadian government has no formal responsibility to provide veterans with the care they required. Harris (2014, 465–7) has mused that Harper switched from celebrating the nation's soldiers as heroes to treating them as second-class citizens when he realized that Canadian support for the Afghan mission was eroding. If so, this is a poignant example of Harper's mindset that the end – political victory – justifies the means.

Nickerson (2014, 24) observes that Harper was "seemingly indifferent" to the horrific human suffering in war and "blithely unmoved by the blood and horror involved." Could this be true? As I well know from personal experience, the expression of grief is both an individual and cultural variable. Harper appears to be an individual who keeps a lid on his emotions. Besides, this is a man who apparently loves hockey, and rumours suggest that he is also fond of cats. How could such a figure be misanthropic?

Ultimately I think that what counts most about Harper may be his Hobbesian/Darwinian world view (Amato 2002) and the extent to which it was implanted in the Conservative Party. For Harper the world seems to be a nasty, brutish place marked by endless struggle, which is assumed to be essential for species survival. Individual success supposedly reflects superior talent, initiative, and sacrifice, and the winners deservedly sit at the head of the table. In this context it would be inappropriate in the extreme *not* to promote the military as an indispensable institution, and *not* to unleash it when threats (real or imagined) to the nation surface. All of this implies that Harper and others who share his mindset are old-fashioned genetic reductionists enamoured with the notion of "the natural order." This is why in the next chapter I'll take a long look at the genetics of war and evolution and reflect on what it tells us about Harper and his politics.

Hillier also appeared at times to lack a sensitivity gauge. Recall his blunt assertions that the business of soldiers is to kill, and the enemy in Afghanistan – the terrorists or insurgents – are "scumbags" (Campion-Smith and Whittington 2008). Perhaps Hillier intended these crude remarks for civilian consumption in order to jolt the public into reality; and perhaps he assumed that his troops were canny enough to realize that the words were not meant for them. It can only be hoped that this was the case. Otherwise Hillier has presented a model for his troops that all too closely resembles the mindset that characterized the erstwhile Airborne regiment.

Let me now try to sum up the impact of Hillier and Harper on Canadian society and how they have fared personally. In 2008 Hillier stepped down as CDS (or, more accurately, was pushed out) and retired from the Armed Forces. As a measure of his impressive career, he was appointed chancellor of Memorial University. In his autobiography he was moved to observe (2009, 500), "The CF is probably our most respected institution these days."

As for Harper, his election defeat at the hands of another Trudeau must have been a bitter pill to swallow. An enigma to the end, he appears to fit the portrait of politicians drawn by the noted political scientist Laswell (see Emmet 1971, 85): flawed individuals suffering from infantile neurosis; actually, this may be one of their strengths, driving them towards their goals regardless of the obstacles. It should be added that, unlike Mulroney, Harper did not leave the Conservatives almost obliterated from the political landscape; the party still did well enough to constitute the parliamentary opposition.

It remains to be seen whether the changes introduced by the Harper government will endure. It is one question whether the Liberals will be able to turn the clock back, and another whether they will want to. They may find that the power accumulated in the PMO and the whittled down clout of Parliament are too seductive for a government to relinquish. As for the Conservatives, there may be a lesson in Liberal history. Pierre Trudeau, a change-oriented prime minister, was followed briefly by John Turner and then the extended housekeeping version of Chrétien. The Conservatives may decide that it is in their long-term interests to embrace a similar pattern of succession in order to consolidate their gains and build trust.

It was Machiavelli in *The Prince* who posed the question whether it is better to be loved or feared. His answer was that their combined impact serves a regime best, but if that is not feasible, then fear is the preferred option. There was a time when Canada enjoyed the respect (love?) of nations around the globe. With its shift to militarism, that no longer was the case, and to the extent that the country became feared, it was because it had hitched its wagon to the imperialist designs of its Western allies.

This does not mean that peacekeeping is dead in Canada. Indeed, the continuing support for peacekeeping (see Buechert 2011, 72) suggests that all of the efforts by Harper and Hillier, and academics such as Granatstein and Bercuson, have failed to make a lasting impression. Anker (2005) acknowledges that the Canadian public remains committed to peacekeeping, which he contends is obsolete, at least in the Pearsonian sense, but laments that Canadians fail to appreciate that the Afghanistan mission represents the dominant peacekeeping operation today. He is correct to the extent that the old distinction between war and peace has collapsed. Since

9/11, armies have been inclined to fashion peace via the barrels of their guns, giving rise to the Orwellian label "peacewarriors." In Anker's opinion, the disconnect between the public's support for peacekeeping and its opposition to the Afghan mission was simply a failure of effective communication by the government and the military. A different interpretation is that the public understood all too well what was transpiring in Afghanistan.

Actually, it would not be surprising if Canadians were confused about their military's presence in Afghanistan, because the government's explanation went through several versions. Harper's first minister of defence, O'Connor, bluntly stated that the mission amounted to revenge for 9/11, implying that force was its defining character. This shifted to a picture of the troops helping to rebuild the country. It was in this context that the vision known as the 3-Ds (defence, diplomacy, and development) was publicized, possibly as a ploy to persuade Canadians that the mission was not so far from peacekeeping after all. Then there was the focus on women and children, certain to draw sympathy back home. And just in case a segment of the Canadian public regretted the shift from aggressive confrontation to humanitarian aid, the old chestnut always remained near at hand: Canada and its allies were taking the fight to the enemy before the enemy sought us out at home. What never could be acknowledged was that Canada's troops were in Afghanistan partly as an exercise in public relations.

Let me close with a recommendation. If Canada really wants to play in the big leagues, why not develop its own nuclear bombs? Surely the military would be pleased, as well as citizens who contend that peacekeeping has had its day in the sun, and just imagine the swagger of some of our political leaders. Most critical of all, our militaristic neighbours to the south no doubt would be absolutely delighted, especially if we opted for those small nuclear bombs that, according to a report in the *International New York Times* (12 January 2016), President Obama was considering adding to his country's arsenal.

part two

Why War?

chapter four

Genetic Basis of War

As stated in the Introduction, this and the next chapter – each of which strives for a deep explanation of war – provide a conceptual foundation for Parts One and Three. What is impressive is the degree to which the genetic and cultural perspectives overlap with each other and together resonate with the ideology and world view of the Canadian Forces and Conservative Party during the Harper decade.

It has often been remarked that war is as old as human society. It has always been with us and always will be. Does this mean that war is innate, natural, embedded in our genetic make-up? One of the most important studies to address this question is *Genetic Seeds of Warfare* by Shaw and Wong (1989). Although they place enormous emphasis on biology and its decisive influence on human interaction throughout history, they do not argue that war is innate. There is no single gene for war, nor even a combination of genes that renders war inevitable. Instead, human beings possess a *propensity* for warfare.

The intellectual tradition that guides *Genetic Seeds of Warfare* is sociobiology. Sociobiology (Wilson 1975) is a multidiscipline and evolutionary framework that embraces both genetics and culture/environment in order to explain the development of human society from its inception to contemporary times. The key distinction for Shaw and Wong is between ultimate and proximate causes. Ultimate causes rest on a genetic base. Proximate causes are expressed in the culture/environment domain. Together they explain why a propensity for warfare has emerged. In this context, the authors are adamant that the old debate about nature versus nurture is obsolete. An analysis based solely on either biology or culture is futile. Only when they are portrayed as complementary can insight and understanding flourish.

At the genetic level, two ultimate causes are fundamental: inclusive fitness and kin selection. Inclusive fitness connotes the conditions that contribute to the health of the organism, in this case the human being. Kin selection concerns the unit of interaction appropriate at different stages of human evolution for the survival of the species. Shaw and Wong label the small tight-knit groups that took shape at the dawn of human society the "nucleus ethnic group." It is their conviction that the roots of this rudimentary form of kinship have been embedded in each successive stage of organized human interaction, including the band, the tribe, and the modern state.

Not surprisingly, Darwin's monumental accomplishments are relevant to the sociobiology project, but Shaw and Wong find his conception of the survival of the fittest inadequate. This is because the great man's unit of analysis is the individual. What is missing is the recognition that survival also operates at the group level. Shaw and Wong define inclusive fitness as an individual *and* kin group phenomenon, and this leads to a very significant distinction: that between egoistic and altruistic motives and behaviour. The insight here is that an organism's inclusive fitness is enhanced if genetically related individuals favour each other over unrelated individuals, and even sacrifice for the benefit of their group. Such "altruistic nepotism," the authors state (Shaw and Wong 1989, 31), is manifested throughout history as the context of kin relatedness is expanded to include ever larger units of organized interaction, culminating in the supra-family connotation of the nation state.

Actually, Shaw and Wong conclude that the basic unit of natural selection is neither the individual nor the kin group. It is even more elementary: the gene (28). The combined impact of ultimate and proximate causes has a single overriding purpose: the survival of the kin's gene pool. Warfare, an expression of ultimate and proximate causes, is said to contribute to this goal.

Although the tendency for human beings to dichotomize the world into us versus them – a pattern reinforced by xenophobia, ethnocentrism, nationalism, and patriotism – has usually been condemned as a source of human misery and misanthropic aggression, Shaw and Wong celebrate it. This is not because they believe human beings *ought* to operate in this manner. Instead their scientific orientation mandates a focus on and recognition of empirical reality, on the world as it is (or as they perceive it). From their perspective, not only is the Us-Them divide universal over time and space, but it also is functional in that it contributes to inclusive fitness.

As soon as nucleus ethnic groups appeared on the scene, xenophobia kicked in. Unrelated ethnic groups were feared and demonized. This happened, according to the authors, because xenophobia is natural; it is hard-wired into the human brain (78). Then there is ethnocentrism, which the authors portray as an outgrowth of xenophobia. As population expanded, ethnocentrism emerged to complement xenophobia in dividing the world into allies and enemies, with kin as the determining factor. The closer people are related genetically, the greater degree of in-group amity and out-group enmity, to the ultimate benefit of inclusive fitness. Put otherwise, confrontations between the in-group and the out-group, even violent ones, have been altogether rewarding for humankind.

Xenophobia and ethnocentrism continued to divide the world into us versus them as social organization passed through hunters and gatherers, clans, tribes, and chiefdoms. By the time large-scale cultural groups and the early stages of the nation state appeared, xenophobia and ethnocentrism became reinforced by what the authors label as two critical psychological identification mechanisms: nationalism and patriotism. Their purpose was to solve the problem of how to implant the nucleus ethnic group into greatly expanded units of social organization. Nationalism was the answer in culturally homogeneous populations. It fused the cultural group to the nation state and portrayed the latter as the family writ large. Culturally heterogeneous populations presented a greater challenge, because culture and state represented different scales, the first being plural and the second singular. In this situation, patriotism emerged to do what nationalism could not in multicultural societies, but it could never be as potent as nationalism, because the vested interests of each of its component parts (nations) potentially competed with the state for identity and allegiance (158–60).

Shaw and Wong recognize that warfare is a cultural phenomenon but explain that it is not a genuine cultural creation. Instead warfare is an expression of the underlying psychological identification mechanisms. These mechanisms are neither purely genetic nor purely cultural, but rather a "dynamic interface" (94) between nature and culture. They emerged to determine the most preferred group membership in order to maximize inclusive fitness as society moved beyond bands, tribes, and chiefdoms; this was none other than the nation state. At the same time these mechanisms identified new targets – other nations – for the in-group's hostility.

In this context, a perplexing question arises: what role does rationality and consciousness play with regard to the identification mechanisms? If rational is taken to be functional, then nationalism and patriotism are rational in that they contribute to inclusive fitness, at least according to the authors. But did human beings consciously adopt these mechanisms, or were they the outcome of genetic/cultural impulses?

Shaw and Wong's views on the working of the human brain elucidate this question (71–6). They reject the notion that the brain is a tabula rasa, an empty vessel filled over time solely by cultural learning and individual experience. Equally important for the brain's operation is instinct. According to the authors the brain is an "enabling mechanism" that not only enhances survival, but also adapts to the evolving interaction between genetic and cultural variability that occurs over time. In other words, the brain too evolves to cope with the new circumstances.[1]

All this is quite complex, but what I think it adds up to is a variation on the idea of system rationality, or functional interdependence of component parts in the service of one or more goals. System rationality is not deliberate or conscious in the sense that actor's rationality is, but it is rational in the sense of logical

Figure 1. Model of Shaw-Wong Framework[2]

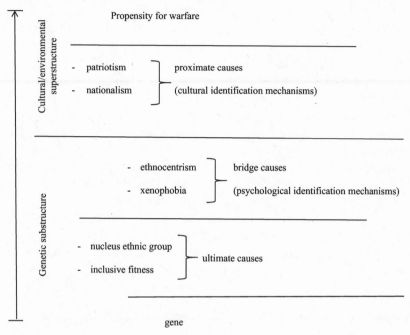

consistency and means appropriate to an ultimate end, in this case the reinforcement of inclusive fitness.

Criticisms

The Shaw-Wong thesis certainly is novel in that it portrays as beneficial what usually is interpreted as harmful. The Us-Them dichotomy, a principal source of hostility and aggression set in motion by xenophobia and ethnocentrism, and sustained by nationalism and patriotism, is presented as the indispensable lever for the survival of the species – not in a moral sense, but rather in terms of its functional contribution.

Eventually, however, a monkey wrench jammed up the conceptual machinery. The monkey wrench was the advent of nuclear weapons. As the authors observe (197), these weapons have been a game changer: "Humans have outfoxed themselves. They have learned to maximize inclusive fitness – through ethnocentrism, out-group enmity, nationalism and patriotism – to the extent that they have created the means to destroy the very inclusive fitness they seek to foster and protect."

Shaw and Wong are quite pessimistic about the prospect of avoiding nuclear annihilation. Neither the United Nations nor peace movements nor religion can remove the danger. The UN is hopeless, because it is an arena of competing vested national interests that mitigate against unified policy and action; in this respect, the UN is a special case of multiculturalism without even the benefit of a mechanism such as patriotism. Grassroots peace movements, in turn, rub against the grain of the power struc-ture, ideology, and interests of the wider society and are readily chewed up and disgorged onto the margins of society. In view of the general thrust of the sociobiological framework, uniform support for the mechanisms that contribute to inclusive fitness (including warfare), rather than pockets of dissent, would have been expected; perhaps peaceniks can be dismissed as poorly socialized citizens. As for religion, according to Shaw and Wong it is not incompatible with war. To the contrary, it is an "enabling mechanism" (188) that reinforces in-group solidarity, ethnocen-trism, and nationalism.

The only hope for the world in the age of potential nuclear war, they suggest, is to divorce nationalism and patriotism from the logic and demands of inclusive fitness. To do so would be to turn their entire trajectory of human history on its head, and the authors have almost nothing to say about how this could be achieved. Their only suggestion is that an international political forum, a world government, might avert disaster – a curious solution, given their previous dismissal of the United Nations as toothless.

An obvious target for criticism is the assumption that the mech-anisms that reinforce the Us-Them dichotomy became dysfunc-tional only in the era of nuclear arsenals. A strong case could be made for the argument that these mechanisms have had a negative impact on human society ever since the formation of nucleus ethnic groups. Only if we accept the assertion that the various iterations of us versus them over the course of history are indispensable for inclusive fitness does the Shaw-Wong model hold water. Even then, in view of the strife and suffering that the Us-Them dynamic has entailed, what a price has been paid.

The authors only occasionally refer to racism, but their model just as readily accounts for a propensity towards racism as it does for warfare; after all, us versus them and xenophobia, ethnocentrism, nationalism, and patriotism are the building blocks of racism. In a now-dated study of organized racism and anti-Semitism in Canada (Barrett 1987), I was intrigued to learn that some of the right-wing organizations had latched onto sociobiology as the ultimate scientific proof of the soundness of their world view.

Actually, there may be an encouraging implication here. Over the past half-century, racial ideology, beliefs, and behaviour have been condemned around the globe. It would be comforting to think that a similar massive transformation in attitudes might undermine the propensity for war. Yet none of us should hold our breath, because pockets of overt racism linger still, not to speak of the covert racism that has been driven underground. Moreover, it is not entirely improbable that future conflicts involving shifts in superpower rivalry, global warming, and a deepening divide between the haves and have-nots will give rise to vestiges of the deranged racial ideologies of the past.

Shaw and Wong express frustration over the tendency of their critics to interpret their approach as biological reductionism. One can almost hear them exclaiming, "What about those proximate causes?" It is correct that they entertain the dual impact of ultimate and proximate causes, but priority is given to the former. The very language – ultimate and proximate – implies that the dice are loaded in favour of genetics, and perhaps the title of the book is suggestive too.

One might also take exception to their portrayal of nationalism and patriotism as mechanisms that emerged to create the nation state. It would be just as plausible to suggest that these mechanisms served to consolidate and legitimate the nation state after it surfaced as a form of social organization.

My final critical comment will not please the authors any more than the preceding ones. Julian Steward (1955), a scientifically oriented anthropologist wed to a cultural ecology and evolutionary perspective, focused on the role of technology on society. When the level of technology is rudimentary, the environment controls social organization and culture. When technology becomes highly advanced, the environment ceases to be influential, and culture emerges as the dominant causal force in society. Could it be argued that in the advanced technological societies of today a similar shift in causality has reversed the relationship between ultimate and proximate causes, with the latter now the ultimate ones and the former reduced to the proximate ones? If so, the genetic base obviously remains intact, but the symbol displaces the gene in terms of impact on contemporary human interaction.[3]

Case Studies

In chapters 6 and 7 Shaw and Wong pause in order to demonstrate the power of their arguments in the context of African coups d'état and a handful of selected states.

They regard coups d'état as a special case of warfare and correctly criticize modernization theory for its naive assumption that tribal and ethnic ties would fade away as economic development, urbanization, and Western forms of education expanded. Yet their insight amounts to little more than stating that persistent tribalism, itself an expression of the deep-rooted nucleus ethnic group, weakens state formation and gives rise to competition for political dominance achieved by coups d'état. One hardly requires the sociobiological framework to arrive at this earth-shattering revelation.

In chapter 7 the potential for and evidence of nationalism and patriotism is examined in Japan, South Africa, Israel, Iran, Afghanistan, United States, and the former USSR. The measuring rod consists of five recognition or identification markers: shared language, common religion, beliefs of common descent, dominant phenotype, and recognized homeland.

Japan is described as a special case, because it scores high on all five identification markers, and its homogeneous culture makes it one of the rare genuine nation states today (as distinct from the multinational state). The authors stress the degree to which Japanese citizens identify with the state and the unifying role of the emperor. Such national unity, combined with Japan's hierarchical social order, is said to account for its tendency towards mobilized aggression and sacrifice and fanaticism in war.

Afrikaners in South Africa also scored high on the identification markers. They shared a common language (a variant of Dutch), a common religion (Calvinism), a common phenotype, and they regard southern Africa as a homeland. What was missing was a creation myth, but Shaw and Wong persuasively argue that "The Great Trek" in the 1800s to the South African interior, prompted by the refusal of the Afrikaners to accept British domination (especially the demand to free their black slaves), crystallized as a creation myth in its own right. Their in-group solidarity, and arguably inclusive fitness, was reinforced by conflict with both the British settlers and the Indigenous population. Contributing to this solidarity was the Afrikaner sense of being a chosen people whose presumed racial superiority mandated a civilizing mission among "the heathen."

Nationalism is well developed in Israel. Israelis share a common religion, a belief in common descent, and a recognized homeland; like the Afrikaners, the belief that they have been the chosen people also is nurtured. However, ethnic and cultural diversity, reflected in the existence of the diverse populations of European Jews (the Ashkenazim) and North African and Middle Eastern Jews (the Sephardim) has posed a threat to the unity of the nation state. It has been overcome partly by the promotion of Hebrew as the national language, as well as by the memory of the Holocaust and sustained conflict with the Arab world. All of this has reinforced Israeli nationalism and promoted a willingness for self-sacrifice and out-group aggression to the ultimate benefit, the authors argue, of inclusive fitness.

Treatment of the next two cases, Iran and Afghanistan, is quite different from the previous three. Iran scores high on all five identification markers: common religion (Shia), language (Farsi), homeland, phenotype, and belief in common descent (Persian). Yet the authors choose to refer to Iranian nationalism as especially violent, fanatical, xenophobic, and racist. Why Iran deserves to be characterized in this negative manner any more than the previous cases is not explained; nor why xenophobia, described over and over as a critical resource for inclusive fitness, suddenly has become transformed into evidence of evil.

The only recognition marker in Afghanistan, according to the authors, is Islam, and even it is divided into the Shia and Sunni branches. This country is described as an arena of competing tribes capable of unified action only by virtue of external threat. The 1979 Soviet invasion certainly qualified as a threat, generating cooperation among factions to eradicate the common enemy. The authors conclude that the best that can be expected in Afghanistan is "tribal nationalism." Yet surely Afghanistan is little different from dozens of current states that historically hosted tribalism. Why, too, did the authors ignore the era of peace, progress, and collective aspirations that thrived in Afghanistan in the decades preceding the Soviet invasion?

It seems obvious that in relation to Iran and Afghanistan the objectivity of the authors was missing. Yet there is a more serious flaw, because it applies to all five case studies. Although the material in each of them is often quite interesting, virtually nothing is added by tying the state to inclusive fitness, which, of course, has been the authors' rationale for the exercise. Furthermore, conventional (non-Marxist) conflict theory revolving around an external threat provides sufficient explanation in itself for internal solidarity without searching for evidence of inclusive fitness.

These cases all concerned nationalism. The final two deal with patriotism in relation to two multi-ethnic societies, the United States and the USSR. The most important distinction made by the authors is between multi-ethnic societies based on immigration and those based on conquest. The United States represents the first type, the USSR the second. The genius of America, the authors argue, has been its success in implanting patriotism despite the absence of a common cultural and ethnic population and a belief in shared descent. A significant source of its success, the authors contend, is the American Constitution, an emotional symbol of unity and loyalty.

In the United States, according to Shaw and Wong, no single ethnic or cultural group is privileged. This predisposes cultural groups to smother their nationalist inclinations and identify with the state. In this regard the fact that immigration to America has been voluntary is important. It arguably renders immigrants more likely to give their allegiance to the state. Of course, the great exception are American blacks. Yet even in their case patriotism is said to be robust. As evidence, the authors point to the high representation of blacks in the armed forces. An alternative explanation for their military participation is the avenue for upward mobility that it represents. Yet the authors counter that the black population realizes that participation in the state's security apparatus enhances their inclusive fitness. In my judgment, there is a much simpler motivation: sheer self-interest and survival.

Because the former USSR evolved through conquest, patriotism was much more elusive. Each separate ethnic and cultural group was prone to developing its own nationalist sentiments rather than identifying with the state. As a counter force, the Soviet state attempted to instil the model of the Soviet patriot as an expression of Marxist-Leninist ideology. However, it was undermined not only by ethnic minority nationalism but also by the dominant nationalism of the Russian ethnic group. In this regard, the authors highlight the privilege enjoyed by White Russians in a supposedly egalitarian society, but that is not substantially different from the advantages enjoyed by white Americans (or Canadians).

The authors conclude that USSR patriotism was essentially Russian nationalism in disguise. Such a situation posed a great danger to the state, because it made room for competing cultural nationalisms to thrive. This is a plausible conclusion, and indeed this entire section on American and USSR patriotism is insightful. My only quarrel with it is the repeated insistence that behind almost everything to do with patriotism lies the issue of inclusive fitness, and the same was true of nationalism. From my perspective, the focus here on inclusive fitness is gratuitous. It amounts to little more than an expression of faith in the sociobiological framework. For this reason, despite some interesting ideas regarding nation states and multinational states, these several case studies only marginally advance the explanatory claims for the multidiscipline and evolutionary model.

Conclusion

Genetic Seeds of Warfare is a highly scholarly and stimulating study, particularly well written in view of its complex subject matter. No doubt many readers will be impressed by its message because of the authoritative aura around science and scientists. In a previous research project (Barrett 1994) I asked a young man in rural Ontario what he thought of a high-profile Canadian scientist and racist who contended that Asians are superior intellectually to whites, who in turn are superior to blacks. Perhaps, the young man mused, the scientist had discovered a gene.

To an extent possibly rivalled only by sex, science sells, whether the product is a set of ideas or soap and toothpaste. No doubt without scientific breakthroughs our lives today would be a great deal more miserable and brutal; just try to persuade diabetics or coronary patients otherwise. In this context, it seems almost indecent to mention the downside: genetically modified food, gas fracking, and the perennial shadow of potential nuclear war.

Science has not always been paramount, nor is it entirely today. Prior to the Age of Reason, scholars turned to theology for answers, and even after the advent of the empirical tradition, anti-scientific movements were not unknown. Throughout recent history, scholarship has oscillated between the culturalization of nature and the naturalization of culture. Whenever a new way of looking at the world crystallizes, in dialectic fashion its opposite begins to dog it. Thus, the Enlightenment with its emphasis on rationality, secularism, and progress produced the counter-Enlightenment with its promotion of subjectivity, spirituality, nationalism, and tradition. More recently, science has been challenged by postmodernism and cultural studies, part of their message being that science itself is a cultural product through and through. *Genetic Seeds of Warfare*, an example of the naturalization of culture, is therefore only one possible way of looking at the history of humankind. While I disagree with critics who accuse it of blatant genetic reductionism, its sociobiological framework, in my judgment, is more speculative than sound.

In view of my criticisms of the *Genetic Seeds of Warfare*, why in the world have I devoted an entire chapter to it? One reason is that it offers a deeper explanation of warfare than most other studies. It also poses a challenge to my own sociocultural biases, which include a tendency to regard biology as a constant that cannot explain the enormous range of variation in beliefs and behaviour around the globe. The fact that it is a scientific approach also has its attraction for me, because the principles of science guide sociocultural anthropology too, even though my discipline lacks the rigour and method to ever live up to them.

All of the above are relevant, but they are almost trivial in comparison to the key significance of the sociobiological framework: its remarkable fit with the world view of Harper's Conservative Party and its glorification of the military. Consider the following: the survival of the fittest, reflected in the assumption that in a healthy society the strong and deserving rise to the top; the accompanying assumption that hierarchy is natural and desirable; the notion that society is a natural system that works best when politics and the state do not interfere with its "laws"; the contradictory assumption that society does not actually exist, only individuals do, which explains the hostility towards sociology; the emphasis placed on nationalism and patriotism; the religiosity of the Conservative faithful; the tendency to identify with one's nucleus ethnic group represented today by Western civilization, a manifestation of the Us-Them dichotomy; the related alignment with NATO and American military adventures, and the hostility towards the United Nations and internationalism in general; Harper's decision to reattach "Royal" to the nation's armed forces; the attacks on the niqab and "barbaric cultural practices" because they are thought to be alien to Western civilization; once again, the Us-versus-Them divide and the survival of the fittest syndrome that mandate a potent military machine and a readiness to deploy it.

What a delicious irony: evangelical Christians like Harper are adamantly opposed to the evolutionary framework and sceptical of science in general, yet their world view unwittingly validates the central arguments in *Genetic Seeds of Warfare*.

chapter five

Cultural Basis of War

A set of ideas does not have to be valid in order to be influential. Consider, for example, the long and pernicious impact of racial classifications based on arbitrary criteria such as skin colour and head shape. The study that will be featured in this chapter, political scientist Samuel Huntington's *The Clash of Civilizations* ([1996] 2003), is in my judgment similarly suspect, but it certainly has made a splash. According to Flynn-Piercey (2011), even Huntington's brief warm-up piece (1993a) on the same theme has been cited more than 10,000 times.

For three reasons *The Clash of Civilizations* has special relevance for my study. First, it offers a novel paradigm for understanding conflict and war in the post–Cold War era. Second, there is a remarkable overlap between Shaw and Wong's *Genetic Seeds of Warfare* and Huntington's *Clash*; indeed, Huntington does for the proximate causes of war what Shaw and Wong do for the ultimate causes. Third, just as the Shaw-Wong perspective coincided with the world view of Harper's Conservative Party and the neoconservative project more generally, the linkage is possibly even more pronounced in Huntington's provocative study.

The key concepts for Huntington are culture and civilization, which he presents as synonyms; culture is defined simply as a way of life, and civilization is the broadest form that culture takes. The author's contention is that in the wake of the Cold War, culture and civilization have displaced ideology, politics, and economics as the principal sources of local and global identity and strife.

Huntington regards as naive the notion that the end of the Cold War opened the door to world harmony and a re-energized United Nations. To the contrary, it left people mentally and emotionally stranded, deprived of their identities based on political ideology. Out of this identity vacuum emerged what the author assumes to be the fundamental human question: "Who are we?" (21). The answer is found in culture, the most meaningful identity for human beings everywhere, at least according to the author. Thus began the trend for people to band together based on shared ancestry, religion, language, and values. At the local level this was manifested in ethnic identity, at the global level in civilizational identity.

It was the turn towards culture, the author asserts, that accounted for the worldwide resurgence of religious fervour. The key element in all civilizations is said to be religion, followed by language. Religion in *Clash* is described as unrivalled in its capacity to motivate and mobilize people. More than anything else, it equips people with a sense of identity and meaning in their lives. Little wonder that religion boils over in so many of the current international hotspots, or that Huntington portrays civilizations as military bodies (128): "In a world where culture counts, the platoons are tribes and ethnic groups, the regiments are nations, and the armies are civilizations." All of this imbues the clash of civilizations with an air of inevitability.

Civilizations are cultural rather than political entities and cannot be equated with race, because a civilization can accommodate multiple races.[1] Although civilizations do change over the long run and the boundaries between them are fuzzy, they are unique in that they outlast governments, ideologies, and empires. As a result of its inherent ethnocentrism, including the dubious assumption that the globe can be divided into civilized and non-civilized peoples, the concept of civilization was discarded long ago by most anthropologists. Yet Huntington writes with confidence that there are currently seven major civilizations, each with its own distinctive religion: Hindu, Islamic, Orthodox, Japanese, Latin American, Western, and Sinic; the last includes China and nations that bear the stamp of its culture such as Taiwan, Singapore, and Korea.[2]

Three other important concepts are core states, fault lines, and cleft countries. According to Huntington each major civilization, with the notable exception of Islam and Latin America (and Africa too, if it is included in the list; see note two) is represented by a dominant state. For example, in Western civilization it is the United States, while in Orthodox civilization it is Russia. In any civilization the core state is the hub for its cultural kin, accounting for the magnetic pull of Canada towards America. With the power of the core state comes not only the privilege of deciding what wars to fight, but also the responsibility of communicating with its civilizational equivalents in order to smother bushfires ignited by their client states before they spread any further.

Fault-line conflicts erupt at the dividing line between civilizations. They represent the greatest danger to the contemporary world, because they potentially mobilize entire civilizations. Cleft (or torn) countries refer to states in which two or more civilizations coexist. The current conflict in Ukraine, the author explains, is especially volatile, because it is both a fault-line confrontation (the Christian West versus the Orthodox East) and a cleft country one (the same split within Ukraine itself). Huntington cautions that only if the United States and Russia decide to lean on their proxies rather than egging them on is a resolution to the Ukraine crisis achievable.

Huntington's forecast (183): "The dangerous clashes of the future are likely to arise from the interaction of Western arrogance, Islamic intolerance, and Sinic assertiveness." He refers (184) to Islam and China as "the challenger civilizations," both of which are convinced that their cultures are superior to the West. By Western arrogance, Huntington essentially means America's assumption that its culture is universal: all nations ought to and eventually will adopt it for their own.[3]

At this juncture, Huntington focuses the analysis on modernization. The disintegration of the Cold War was not the only source of alienation and impetus for new forms of identity. Modernization was its partner in crime. The anchors of family, clan, and village all become dislodged as a result of urbanization, education, social mobility, increased media consumption, and awareness of and contact with other civilizations. Culture, as we have seen, rushed in to fill the void – especially its main element, religion.

Huntington draws a sharp distinction between modernization and Westernization, and argues that the former does not necessarily mean the latter. Indeed, the reality may be precisely the opposite (78): "In fundamental ways, the world is becoming more modern and less Western." At the heart of this dynamic are the different value systems of America and other civilizations. Asians, for example (275), emphasize the Confucian values of "authority, hierarchy, the subordination of individual rights and interests, the importance of consensus, the avoidance of confrontation ... and the supremacy of the state over society." Americans stress "liberty, equality, democracy and individualism" while at the same time opposing authority and promoting competition and human rights. While Asians are comfortable with the prospect of long-term gains, Americans demand instantaneous reward for their efforts (on page 319 a similar contrasting portrait is provided of Singapore values). Huntington aptly captures what all this signifies (184): "What is universalism to the West is imperialism to the rest."

This brings us to the author's fixation on Islam. Far from rejecting modernization, the Islamic Resurgence, as Huntington labels it, is both a product of the alienating impact of modernization and an effort to move Muslim societies further along the path to modernity. The Islamic Resurgence represented a roadmap whose starting point was Islamic history and culture rather than the model of the West.

I now turn to some of Huntington's controversial assertions about Islam. He begins reasonably enough, pointing out that when the Cold War fizzled out, the West and Islam lost their common enemy, communism, and rediscovered the ancient enmity between them. Exacerbating this state of affairs was the absence of a key state within Islam, with which the West might have been able to establish a dialogue. This absence, according to Huntington, is partly responsible for tension and conflict both within Islamic societies and with the outside world.

More provocative is the author's observation (217) that Islam is a civilization "whose people are convinced of the superiority of their culture and obsessed with the inferiority of their power." Guaranteed to raise the ire of Muslims are two other assertions: "Whenever one looks along the perimeter of Islam, Muslims have problems living peacefully with their neighbours" (256). And "Islam's borders are bloody, and so are its innards" (258). By innards, Huntington is again reminding us that Muslim societies are racked by internal strain. He remarks that no other statement in his 1993 article drew more anger than this one, but he continues to insist that nobody, Muslim or non-Muslim, can deny the reality of Muslim bellicosity.

Huntington reviews six possible causes of Muslim violence (262–5). First, the aggression built into Islam, the religion of the sword, with its glorification of military virtues. Second, the expansion of Islam across North Africa, the Middle East, central Asia, and the Balkans, complemented by the expansion of the Russian Empire. In this way Islam was brought face to face with different civilizations, which in Huntington's view is a recipe for confrontation rather than mutual benefit.

Third, "the indigestibility" of Muslims. This is a highly loaded charge, and to the author's credit he points out that non-Muslims are just as indigestible to Muslims. He describes Islam as an absolute faith that blends together religion and politics and aims to create a community of true believers that surmounts and minimizes national boundaries. It is this universalistic tendency in Islam that supposedly creates havoc. Of course, universalism is also embedded in Christianity, because it, along with Islam, is one of the two main proselytizing world religions. Later it will be indicated that Huntington is just as scathing about Western, especially American, universalism as he is about Islam's.

Fourth, Western imperialism. When Muslim societies were overrun by the West in the nineteenth and twentieth centuries, the consequences mirrored those that have affected colonial subjects everywhere: a loss of confidence and eventually protest, rage and sometimes violent resistance.[4] We have already encountered the fifth possible cause, the absence of a core state within Islam that could encourage internal order and enhance communications with other civilizations.

The final potential cause is in Huntington's judgment by far the most critical of all: the demographic explosion within Islam. The birth rate of Muslims, according to Huntington, dwarfs that in other civilizations, especially the West. Particularly treacherous both for Muslims and non-Muslims, he argues, is the huge bulge of young, often unemployed males. But there is hope. Huntington speculates (265) that as Muslim societies age, violence within them and towards non-Muslims will decrease. Indeed, he suggests that by the third decade of this century, Islam may cease to be a threat to international harmony. Whether Huntington himself really believes his encouraging forecast is unclear, because he also suggests (65) that in the long run Islam will win out over the Christian West. This is because the latter spreads primarily by conversion while Islam spreads by conversion and reproduction – the demographic factor once again.

Huntington is impressibly erudite, and at times he writes with admirable objectivity. He candidly admits that America is a declining power, although it will remain the dominant state for a long time ahead. He also remarks that the greatest threat today is American aggression, a direct outgrowth of the assumption that its way of life is (or should be) universal. Such universalism, Huntington contends, harms everyone. It infuriates people in other civilizations, who then embrace negative images of America.

While Huntington emphasizes that we now live in a multicultural world – by which he means a world dominated by the seven major civilizations, not a world in which multiculturalism thrives within individual states – he insists that there never has been and never will be a single universal civilization. Unless America gives up its universalist tendencies, the author argues, it will continue to flounder as resentment breeds in the rest of the world. Although Huntington never explicitly urges an isolationist policy for his country, that is the unspoken message in his analysis.

So much for objectivity. Just as Shaw and Wong veered towards Western partisanship when they focused on their case studies, Huntington's biases became astonishingly evident in the last pages of his book. There he turns his wrath against multiculturalism in Western society generally and America specifically. He bluntly asserts that multiculturalism is incompatible with Western civilization, and he worries that minority groups such as Muslims in Europe and Hispanics in the United States who reject assimilation will create cleft nations, with strife and disunity the unavoidable consequences. He also laments the shift in America away from individual rights and towards group rights. It is revealing that he not only fails to produce authoritative sources or data to support his claim about Hispanic opposition to assimilation, but he also ignores the emphasis Shaw and Wong place on patriotism as the mechanism that welded America's various ethnic groups into a collective whole.

Huntington states (318), "A multicultural America is impossible because a non-Western America is not American." Even more strongly (307): "The future of the United States and the West depend upon Americans reaffirming their commitment to Western civilization. Domestically this means rejecting the siren calls of multiculturalism." If Huntington's almost emotional rejection of multiculturalism and group rights does not land him alongside the Republican Party and endear him to neoconservatives, I don't know who else would want to claim him. His views in these final pages of his book prompt the reader to re-evaluate almost everything he wrote earlier.

With the caveat that both American and Muslim society are complex and heterogeneous in beliefs and behaviour, ironically there appear to be a great many similarities between at least a significant portion of their members. Concern about moral decline has been common to both. The Islamic Resurgence (98) was a reaction against secularism and anomie, and expressed a thirst for order, discipline, and solidarity. America's decline, in Huntington's view (304), also has less to do with its shrinking economic power than moral laxness, reflected in high crime rates and the weakening of family bonds and the work ethic. The solution, as we saw, essentially was the reaffirmation of America's unique Western identity.

Muslims and Americans also are alike in their religiosity. Probably no other Western state can match America in church and temple attendance and confessions of faith. It might be suggested that in this society of immigrants from all corners of the globe, religion is the indispensable glue that holds it together. Yet Canada is also a society of immigrants, but it is a great deal more secular than America and much less given to overt expressions of patriotism.[5] It may be that a superpower, an empire, is so complex and cumbersome that it requires a blending potion (an opiate?) over and beyond patriotism (and war); or perhaps it is the nature of an empire to express its superiority not only materially and militarily but also spiritually. Of course, a much simpler explanation might be equally persuasive: the prominence of religion dating back to colonial America, and the tendency to fuse religion and freedom as one of the defining features of the American project. Last but certainly not least is the shared propensity for violence. Huntington has made much of Islamic violence, but in this regard America does not have to take a back seat. In the name of freedom and protection from the bad guys, America flexes its muscles whenever it perceives a need or an opportunity. For friends of America, the world is consequently safer. For its enemies and sometimes even its allies, the world is rendered more fragile and precarious.

This is the appropriate place to expand on the critical reaction to *The Clash of Civilizations*. As indicated earlier, most anthropologists, armed with their relativism, have rejected the civilization concept as ethnocentric. It especially is an assault on that part of the world – mostly small-scale societies – that falls outside the boundaries of Huntington's seven civilizations; arguably these small-scale societies are actually the civilized ones if measured by human virtues such as family and community solidarity and the fusion of the spiritual and natural realms.

Even the term *culture* has been put under the microscope and found to be toxic. At the exact time that Huntington published his 1993 article, the perennial definition of culture as "a way of life" was being challenged as simplistic and deceptive; the charge in part was that it exaggerated homogeneity, timelessness, and uniqueness in "anthropological societies" while obfuscating their implied inferiority and impotence relative to the developed world (see Barrett 2002, 5).

In a piece published just after 9/11, Edward Said (2001) rebuked Huntington for crude abstractions such as the West, Islam, Christianity, civilization, and cultural identity while glossing over internal complexity. Of course, it could be retorted that Said's powerful study, *Orientalism* (1979), is also a gross generalization. How else to characterize an argument that no Westerner's contact with, ideas about, or actions in the Orient, regardless whether they are meant to be benign or malicious, can escape the contaminating impact of the colonial project called Orientalism? As for internal complexity, Huntington occasionally alludes to it, but as in the case of Hispanics in America, his tendency is to condemn it as evidence of a disruptive cleft society.

Huntington gives the impression that hostility between civilizations is almost natural, an expression of the deeply rooted Us-Them paradigm that pervaded *Genetic Seeds of Warfare*. Sato's words (1997) are closer to the truth. He points out that different civilizations not only clash with each other but also learn from and revitalize each other.

In a popular piece in the *New York Times* (2011), David Brooks took exception to Huntington's assertion that Muslims are not nationalistic or in favour of democracy. Certainly Huntington gave the impression that "borderless" Islam left little room for nationalism, and he bluntly stated (29) that Islamic culture is a barrier to democracy. Brooks's further criticism that Huntington ignores the existence of universal values is essentially but not absolutely correct, because our political scientist (318) does allow for the existence of a thin veneer of general values such as the rules against murder and torture. A somewhat similar charge is that Huntington focuses on the religious identity of Muslims to the exclusion of everything else. Yet he does acknowledge (128) that everyone has multiple identities, including family, occupation, and education. This qualification, however, is overwhelmed by the enormous influence that he attributes to culture and civilization, the central element of which is religion.

Not all of the criticisms against Huntington stand up to scrutiny. Brooks also accuses him of overlooking the continuing importance of the state and national interests in the era of cultural dominance. The short response is that he didn't. He insisted (34) that states will still be front and centre in world affairs, even though their interests will be determined by their civilizational roots. Then, too, balance of power initiatives, according to the author (128), will still produce state alliances across different civilizations.

Another criticism is that Huntington ignored conflict *within* Muslim society. Although it is true that his focus is overwhelmingly on strain between Islam and other civilizations, he did recognize that the lack of a dominant state and the presence of large numbers of aimless young men posed both an internal and external threat.

While Shaw and Wong's genetic paradigm is by definition time-less, the possibility of nuclear war notwithstanding, Huntington's claims for the civilizational paradigm are much more modest. He advises that it was not appropriate during the era of the Cold War, and sometime in the future social change will certainly render it obsolete. But if that is so, how do we interpret these words (40): "Human history is the history of civilizations." Unless human his-tory only began after the Berlin Wall came down, Huntington's paradigm too purports to be timeless.

Early in his book (37) and on the final page (321), Huntington congratulated Pearson for his astute recognition of the emerging clash of civilizations, and he quotes the Canadian diplomat's warn-ing (1955, 83–4) that if the clash is to be avoided, "different civiliza-tions will have to learn to live side by side in peaceful exchange, studying each other's history and ideals and art and culture." Both Pearson and Huntington regard inter-civilizational strain as a chal-lenge to be overcome, but there is a nuanced difference between them. Unlike Huntington, Pearson adds a taste of honey; not only is the rebirth of a confident and powerful Orient welcomed, but indeed the prospect of meaningful interaction across civilizations is exhilarating, a source of enrichment for all of humanity.

Let me wrap this section up by focusing more sharply on the overlap between Shaw and Wong's *Genetic Seeds of Warfare* and Huntington's *The Clash of Civilizations*. With the important exception that Huntington does not reduce his analysis to the level of genet-ics, the similarity between his perspective and Shaw and Wong's is quite remarkable, as these quotations from *The Clash* illustrate:

1.   "People are always tempted to divide the world into us and them, the in-group and the other, our civilization and those bar-barians" (32).
2.   "People define their identity by what they are not" (67).

3. "It is human to hate. For self-definition and motivation humans need enemies" (130).
4. "A civilization is an extended family" (156).
5. "Identity at any level – personal, tribal, racial, civilizational – can only be defined in relation to an 'other,' a different person, tribe, race or civilization" (129).
6. "The civilizational 'us' and the extracivilizational 'them' is a constant in human history" (129).
7. "Civilizations are the ultimate human tribes, and the clash of civilizations is tribal conflict on a global scale" (207).
8. "Wars between clans, tribes, ethnic groups, religions, communities, and nations have been prevalent in every era and in every civilization because they are rooted in the identities of people" (252).
9. And in Huntington's early response to his critics entitled "If Not Civilizations, What?" (1993b): "What ultimately counts for people is not political ideology or economic interest. Faith and family, blood and belief, are what people identify with and what they will die for."

If the genetic and cultural frameworks are conceptually similar, and if the former overlaps significantly with the world view of Harper's version of conservatism, it follows logically that the latter probably does as well. The implication is that every example in the previous chapter of the close fit between *Genetic Seeds of Warfare* and the ideology of the Conservative Party is equally applicable to *The Clash of Civilizations*.

Huntington expressed regret (309) that the Clinton administration had failed to appreciate that the clash of civilizations has invaded global politics; it was this same naivety, in the author's opinion, that led to the acceptance of Turkey and then Bosnia as members of NATO. Yet surely the election of George W. Bush and 9/11 made all the difference. On the surface, not necessarily so. Certainly it would be surprising if the 2001 terrorist attack in New York was not interpreted by a great many Americans as undeniable evidence for the clash. Yet the fact is that President Bush repeatedly insisted that his fight was not with Islam, but only with those bad guys, the jihadists, whose actions had contaminated and diminished an otherwise admirable religion.

A Canadian political scientist, Mark Salter (2003), helps to clear up the confusion. There is no doubt in his mind that the Bush administration did adopt Huntington's paradigm as a blueprint for its foreign policy. The reason why Bush praised Islam, he argues, was to discourage Muslim countries from banding together to pose a civilizational front against America's aggression. Salter speculates that the American government launched the open-ended War on Terror and encouraged a sense of fear and danger in order to provide a green light for its attacks on foreign "barbarians" and to justify harnessing its foreign policy to its military might.[6]

Huntington pointed out (248–9) that Muslims had little doubt that the invasion of Iraq was at its core a war of civilizations. Quite possibly he interpreted 9/11 and Bush's reaction as vindication for his thesis. He might even be forgiven in the circumstances if he overlooked his own advice about the necessity of avoiding military excursions in other civilizations, and the importance for America's future of jettisoning its universalistic (civilizing?) inclinations.[7]

Former Canadian prime minister Joe Clark (2013, 37), while recognizing that cultural identity has become tangled in issues of international conflict, nevertheless expressed scepticism about the inevitability of the clash of civilizations. Clark did not explain why he was sceptical, but on purely logical grounds – the overlap between the works of Shaw-Wong and Huntington, the political resonance of the clash of civilizations paradigm in America, and Canada's subordinate role within American hegemony – it follows that Canada too subscribed to Huntington's model. Less abstract evidence is reflected at least faintly in Prime Minister Harper's decision to re-attach "Royal" to the Canadian Forces, and even more revealingly in his creation of the Office of Religious Freedom in 2013; more revealingly, because of the critical role attributed by Huntington to religion for civilizational identity.

It should be added that under Harper's leadership not only was the Canadian military significantly expanded, but in addition the country was a willing partner in the West's military forays abroad. Indeed, it sometimes seemed as if the Conservative Party, often with the support of the Liberals and only to a somewhat lesser extent the NDP, was more eager than its allies to lock horns with its civilizational rivals, Russia and Ukraine being a prime example. Such Canadian bellicosity may not have been so apparent had George W. Bush rather than President Obama occupied the White House during the second half of Harper's tenure. Despite the often-expressed disappointment about Obama's middle-of-the-road leadership, one can only wonder what the world would be like today if Canada under Harper, not America under Obama, had been the globe's superpower during this past turbulent decade.

The Anthropologist's War

We should have seen it coming: the military's infatuation with anthropology in the wake of 9/11. If culture has emerged as the defining characteristic in international relations and war itself, as Huntington contended, why not recruit the recognized cultural experts – anthropologists – for the Iraq and Afghanistan theatres? Enter Montgomery McFate, an American anthropologist. In a co-authored paper in 2005 she made a case for embedding anthropologists with the military in order to reduce cultural barriers between the occupiers and the occupied, in the process helping to win the hearts and minds of the Afghans and Iraqis and dimming their attraction to the insurgency movements.

Within a year the curiously named Human Terrain System (HTS) had been organized in which civilians, preferably trained in anthropology, operated alongside military personnel (Sims 2015). "Human Terrain" is military jargon for a battleground's civilian population; the HTS's job was to map it, with special emphasis on its leaders. In 2007 the first Human Terrain Teams (HTT) were deployed in Iraq and Afghanistan, eventually expanding to more than thirty teams. Each team usually consisted of three military personnel and two civilians equipped (supposedly) with cultural expertise.

The initial reaction beyond anthropology to the HTS program was enthusiastic. Secretary of Defence Robert Gates was a supporter, as eventually was General Pretaeus, and the American media led the cheering back home. The motives of civilians who signed up with HTS were various. Some were moved by altruism, the prospect of injecting a humane dimension into the enterprise of war. The early claims of the impact of their presence must have been gratifying: violent ("kinetic" in military-speak) encounters between the American Forces and the occupied populations reportedly occurred less frequently, and fewer Americans and local citizens were being killed.

Sheer patriotism was another motive, especially for individuals who believed that it was their duty to provide unconditional support when their country was at war. Two further inducements undoubtedly concerned the dismal employment prospects of anthropologists and other social scientists as well as the exceptional financial incentive. Anthropology departments continued to churn out graduates who had little prospect of entering the conventional career path of teaching and research. Applied anthropology outside academia was an optional path, and probably some candidates viewed HTS in this light. Yet the key attraction may well have been the salary that went with a position in HTS: $200,000 plus per annum, with additional perks when decommissioned.

The critical response to HTS among professional anthropologists surfaced so quickly and forcefully as to suggest that it was either an ideologically inspired knee-jerk reaction or indisputable evidence that the rot in the program was so overwhelming that it could be smelled a mile away. In 2007, the same year the first Human Terrain Teams were launched, the American Anthropological Association (AAA) publicly announced (2007) that HTS was an "unacceptable application of anthropological expertise." That also was the year that the Network of Concerned Anthropologists was established to resist militarization of the discipline. A key criticism concerned ethics. Not only did the Human Terrain Teams fail to obtain anything that would pass as consent by research review boards, but indeed there was coercion in the interview process by virtue of the disproportionate power between the occupied and the occupier.[8] Then too, there was an element of secrecy about the information generated by HTS teams, because it fed into the intelligence bank of the military, rather than being released to public scrutiny;

it would be astounding if this information was not absorbed into "the kill chain" of military operations.

Another criticism was that the HTS program was grossly incompetent and ineffective. It supposedly was led by teams of cultural specialists, but few anthropologists took the bait, and only a handful of those who did so had advanced degrees (Price 2011; Fenton 2010). The result was that almost any individual who had a smattering of social science training was brought on board, including political scientists, psychologists, and historians. Virtually none of the recruits possessed the local knowledge and language skills necessary for meaningful research. It is thus not surprising that when Price (2011, 96–7), one of the founders of the Network of Concerned Anthropologists, challenged an army colonel's claim that HTS was a stunning success, reducing combat operations by a remarkable 60 per cent, the military representative had to admit that his claim was based on an impression rather than hard data.

A third criticism came at HTS from quite a different direction. This was the charge that the program was essentially immoral, because the wars in Afghanistan and Iraq (especially the latter) were odious adventures in neocolonialism. Significantly, even the AAA, an organization that sometimes has ditched its ethical principles in order to curry favour with the state,[9] implied in its 2007 "Statement" that the War on Terror being fought in Iraq and Afghanistan was unjust, characterized by "a denial of human rights and based on faulty intelligence and undemocratic principles."

In 2008, no doubt after a thorough evaluation of the benefits and costs of HTS, the Canadian military established its own version of the program with an equally cumbersome title: the White Situational Awareness Team (WSAT). In military terminology, red represents the enemy, blue the friendly forces, and white the civilian population (Forte 2008; Fenton 2010; Bray 2011). Intended for the Kandahar mission, one of the rationales for WSAT was that increased cultural understanding would reduce collateral damage – a splendid euphemism for the slaughter of civilians.[10]

Like the Human Terrain Teams, the Canadian version also consisted of five members, but there were differences. First, only two of the members were military personnel. Second, the three civilians were employees in the Department of Foreign Affairs rather than non-government academics or ersatz cultural experts pulled off the street. This difference should have defused some of the concerns among professional anthropologists about the abuse of their discipline, but criticism in Canada was just as prompt and robust as in America. The man of the hour was a Concordia University scholar, Maximilian Forte. This obviously was a cause close to his heart, because he was tireless in his opposition to WSAT, churning out an endless stream of criticism. He also founded an organization called Anthropology for Justice and Peace, as well as Zero Anthropology, an online organ devoted to undermining the efforts to militarize anthropology, and was a key figure on a panel dealing with the topic at the 2009 annual meetings of the Canadian Anthropological Society held that year in Montreal.

With the termination in 2011 of Canada's Afghanistan mission ("mission" with its religious connotation being a rather peculiar term for war, but not altogether inappropriate in view of the frequent claim that God has blessed it, and in an era where the distinction between warriors and peacekeepers has been fudged), WSAT too was history. Then in 2014 the HTS program was mothballed. Whether or not the relentless criticism in both nations was a factor is an open question. According to a spokesperson for the American military (see Jaschik 2015), HTS was dismantled simply because of the withdrawal of American Forces from Afghanistan and Iraq. This is quite plausible, because it appears that militaries, with their institutional proximity to the core of state power, are relatively immune to public protest, except when it traumatizes an entire nation, such as in America during the final years of the Vietnam War, and perhaps in the former Soviet Union as its invasion of Afghanistan dwindled to an inglorious demise.

The implication is that the message of the critics of HTS and WSAT resonated primarily with their own colleagues rather than with the military. If the critics were effective, it was in defending the integrity of the discipline in its time of need. This itself was a worthwhile achievement, and possibly the more realistic and sophisticated of the critics never expected much more from their efforts.

In similar fashion, it might be suggested that the American and Canadian militaries never seriously believed that culturally sensitive teams could soften the impact of war. The real purpose of HTS, as González has pointed out (2015), may have been its propaganda value: the portrayal of the Iraq and Afghanistan occupations as warfare with a conscience, the kind of combat that citizens back home could proudly embrace.

There have been previous programs in which the state has recruited academics for military and subversive ventures. One was Project Camelot. In 1963 the American Army Office of Research and Development laid plans during the Cold War to monitor and disrupt civil protest and revolution in the Third World. The wheels fell off two years later when Chilean officials and academics learned about the plan and sounded the alarm. Curiously, not all of the potential social science participants were right-wingers. Horowitz, for example, who produced the major autopsy of Project Camelot (1967), was a prominent sociologist on the academic left. He lamented the collapse of the venture, because in his opinion it was a missed opportunity to demonstrate to the government the relevance and importance of social science.

An even more odious venture was launched during the Vietnam War as a counterinsurgency (COIN) initiative.[11] This was Civil Operations and Revolutionary Development Support (CORDS), which employed interviewers to interrogate civilians in Vietnam in order to finger those who sympathized with the Viet Cong. Apparently CORDS operated in conjunction with what was called the Phoenix Program, which undertook to neutralize (i.e., infiltrate, capture, and assassinate) the sympathizers. According to González (2009, 28), fully 26,000 civilians ended up dead as a result of COIN. It might be protested that even in wars considered just, atrocities come with the territory. In unjust wars, ethical lapses are less forgivable.

One further dimension of the military's impact on academia cannot be ignored: its financial penetration. In 2008 a Defence Department program in America called Minerva was announced by Secretary Gates; its mandate was to fund university research topics and programs of interest to the U.S. military. Predictably, university administrators apparently welcomed the funding windfall with open arms, while among the faculty questions were raised about undue influence and the possible loss of scholarly independence (see Price 2011, 60). As McKay and Swift (2012, 281–2) have revealed, the situation in Canada has been little different: "Millions of dollars from Canadian taxpayers are funneled through the DND to universities and platoons of pundits."

Funding for centres of higher learning has always been dicey. In colonial times, anthropologists from wealthy families sometimes financed their own expeditions or were supported by well-heeled patrons. Others were often dependent on their nation's Colonial Office for fieldwork support and eventually on philanthropic organizations such as the Ford Foundation and royal societies. In the decades following the end of colonialism, philanthropic funding remained important, while support from Colonial Offices was replaced by government-sponsored research programs such as the Social Sciences and Humanities Research Council of Canada (SSHRC). In recent years there has been a dramatic change. As Giroux has documented (2007), funding now is likely to flow from corporations and the military, with all that implies about academic freedom and control. Of course, the proverbial man and woman on the street, influenced by the urban myth about the social scientist who received a handsome research grant to locate a local whorehouse, might well manage to suppress their sympathy.

It is commonplace to refer to the First World War as the chemist's war, and the Second World War as the physicist's war. Much to the chagrin of anthropologists (at least most of them, if the AAA's condemnation can be taken as representative of the discipline),[12] with the insertion of HTS into the Iraq and Afghanistan theatres, the War on Terror has become labelled the anthropologist's war.

As indicated earlier, one main criticism mounted by anthropologists concerns ethics, and with good reason. The discipline has come a long way since the era when Nadel (1939) could escape censure for his recommendation that bullying be resorted to when dealing with uncooperative informants. Probably most of us would agree with Price (2011, 199) that our primary loyalty should be to the people we study, and our fundamental aim should be to do them no harm. Yet the picture is not as clear as these principles imply. What happens to our ethical purity when we study up? Do we still owe those in power our loyalty, and honour the duty of doing no harm? Ironically, one possible answer, the correct one in my judgment, is provided by Price's own work, which is an example of studying up, because its main focus is on the powerful. Virtually everything Price has to say about HTS and the occupations of Iraq and Afghanistan repudiates his statement of ethics. He certainly does not offer his loyalty, and to the extent that his criticisms have been effective, they have harmed the HTS program and the military itself. Bravo![13]

There also appears to be an understandable self-serving motive among those of us who find the HTS program weak on ethics. This is revealed in the concern expressed by anthropologists that we may develop a reputation as spies, which could compromise our future fieldwork and even expose us to danger. If so, this would be nothing new. The suspicion that anthropologists are spies has dogged the discipline since colonial times.

There is an old saying that all is fair in love and war, which almost certainly is not true, because there are codified and informal rules of conduct for both the lovelorn and the soldier. What can be observed is that the military's perspective on ethics often stands in contrast with academia and civilian life in general. Reflect on Sun Tzu's emphasis on deception: When you are strong, pretend you are weak; when you are ready to advance, give the impression you are preparing to retreat; and by all means employ spies (in his final chapter he discusses five types), especially those in the service of the enemy who, if captured and converted, can turn the tide of war. This does not mean that military ethics is an oxymoron. Remember those several admirable virtues championed by the military such as loyalty, duty, courage, and honour.

Clausewitz contended that war is different from any other human activity, which Hillier confirmed with his blunt assertion that the job of soldiers is to kill people. Except in some cases such as self-defence and euthanasia, and in countries where the death penalty still exists, war is the only setting where murder is openly legitimized by the state. In this context, Sun Tzu's emphasis on deception carries the aura of the normal. The implication is that the gap in ethics between the military and civilian life cannot be explained at the level of individuals. Instead it is a cultural and institutional phenomenon.

Any evaluation of HTS would be flawed if the ethical issues were ignored, but it can be neatly subsumed within a much broader issue – neocolonialism – which brings us to the tricky distinction between just and unjust wars. Although the horrific First World War might be labelled unjust by some people, because it amounted to a contest between imperial powers, that is not how the American Anthropological Association saw it. In 1919 no less a figure than Franz Boas, the celebrated founder of American anthropology, publicly condemned four archaeologists who had hidden behind their professional credentials to carry out espionage. Almost immediately Boas was censored by the AAA (Price 2011, 17–18), which presumably never would have happened if the war had been regarded as unjust.

There was much less disagreement about the morality of the Second World War, at least from the Allied perspective, because its targets were the Nazis and the Fascists. According to Johannsen (1992, 72) about 90 per cent of American anthropologists joined the war effort. In Britain numerous qualified and prospective anthropologists such as Leach, Fortes, and Goody, all of whom were destined to enjoy sterling careers at Cambridge, and Evans-Pritchard and Bailey (my eventual mentor) at Oxford, signed up for military service. Unlike the recruits for HTS, these men were genuine cultural experts, many of whom became intelligence officers, some of them deployed among the ethnic groups that they had studied first-hand. Their mandate was not to soften the impact of war (except when their adopted ethnic groups bore its brunt) or foster amity across the front lines. Instead it was to hasten the defeat of the enemy.

Apparently when HTS was on the verge of being scrapped, its members searched desperately but unsuccessfully for alternative applications of its "expertise." Would UN peacekeeping missions have fit the bill? Although presumably there would be no ethical objection to HTS participation, at least if its advertised benevolence

were accepted as genuine, its contribution would be largely superfluous, because in a sense UN peacekeepers themselves are cultural brokers.

Actually, there is a setting where HTS could be effective and
beneficial: the university campus. Feuds and vendettas among
faculty members generated by paradigmatic rivalry, personality clashes and sheer envy thrive in academia, and are especially
vicious because of, not despite, the triviality of the issues.[14] Of
course, there are various types of dispute-settling mechanisms on
campus, but similar to feuds in the classical tradition, squabbles in
academia may be suppressed, but with the passage of time they
often boil over again. Human Terrain Teams, having survived the
ordeal of fire, so to speak, in war zones, might well bring to the
table a novel mediating style. Being natives and university graduates means that they would possess the necessary linguistic and
cultural competency, and let us assume that the heavy hit in their
pocketbooks would not be a disincentive. Even their former connection to the centre of power need not be an obstacle, because
most academic feuds that get out of hand are taken over by the
administration, which would no doubt recognize HTS members as
fellow travellers and welcome them aboard.

Quite possibly many citizens of the West and further afield, hor-
rified by the spectre of 9/11 and sympathetic to America's quest for
retaliation, would dismiss the concerns within anthropology about
ethics and neocolonialism as irrelevant ivory-tower nonsense. To
do so would be to fail to grasp the essence of programs like HTS
and WSAT. They are nothing less than the products of asymmetrical wars and indeed are unlikely to pop up elsewhere, as the cases
of the First and Second World Wars illustrated. There is an almost
inevitable progression in asymmetrical wars. First comes the occupation, then insurgency, finally counter-insurgency. Only when the
last stage has been reached are the conditions propitious for an
initiative such as HTS. It is a tool appropriate solely for the powerful, a luxury that insurgents cannot afford. If they could, almost by
definition there would be no insurgency; instead there would be an
indeterminate battle between opponents closely matched enough
to do damage to each other.

Conclusion

There is no lack of candidates in addition to genetics and culture
for the dubious honour of turning humans from peace to war. The
more obvious ones include ideology, territorial expansion, population pressure, power-hungry individuals, the military-industrial
armaments complex, and in earlier times competition for women
and male rites of passage. My focus here will be on some of the less
obvious candidates: revenge, shame, boredom, and beauty.

Revenge, according to Turney-High ([1949] 1971, 149–50), is a
fundamental motive for going to war. Stewart and Strathern (2002,
6) not only concur but also claim that revenge has been a universal impulse for violence in all societies throughout recorded history; indeed it is a thing in itself, not a reaction to anything else, as
deeply embedded in the nature of *Homo sapiens* as Freud's sex and
aggression. In this context remember Defence Minister O'Connor's
observation that it was primarily revenge for 9/11 that landed
American troops in Afghanistan.

With apologies to Stewart and Strathern, there may be something more elementary than revenge: shame. As Gilligan has persuasively argued (1996 and 2004), it is humiliation that ignites the
burning desire for revenge. He arrived at this insight after years of
studying violence in prison. When a prisoner is "dis'd" (shamed),
he is consumed by a single goal, retribution, regardless of the consequences. It is not too much of a stretch to spot humiliation as a
dominant emotion in America during the aftermath of 9/11, an
unbearable insult to the world's most powerful nation.

We now come to Turney-High's controversial ideas about the
motives for war. His main argument (142) is that "times of peace
are often boring," while "war is the most exciting exercise in the
world." He also suggests that individuals are drawn to war in order
to escape the frustrations in their lives. In his words (141), "War is
one of the most effective devices ever invented for this cathartic
purpose." Possibly most startling of all is this comment (166): "A
fact that some people have failed to realize is that war is fun." It was
partly the portrayal of the soldier's life as a lark – rappelling down
from the rafters of arenas during hockey games – that hardened

the resistance of critics to the military's presence at sports events. These critics demanded a more realistic image of war, one that did not sanitize brutality and destruction.

Turner-High's study, originally published in 1949, was one of the early notable works on war by an anthropologist, and although his sunny portrayal of war may be partly true, it is not the whole truth, or even most of the truth, and that may explain why it has largely been ignored in the discipline.

Who would have imagined that war could stimulate an aesthetic experience? Well, wrap your mind around this passage by our prominent historian David Bercuson (1996, 28): "It is the awful beauty of tracer fire at night, of a horizon lit by the gun flashes of a thousand field pieces, of a formation of hundreds of bombers droning through the sky despite bursts of anti-aircraft fire and the wanton attacks of enemy fighters." When I first read this passage, I thought that the author's perception of war was no more realistic than Turney-High's, but then I came across these words written by Martin Bell (1996, 256), a war reporter for BBC television: "A battle at night can be a thing of terrible beauty." Not only was Bell renowned for his coverage of wars around the globe, including Vietnam and Bosnia, but unlike Bercuson his politics were leftish and he actually regarded war as barbaric. Like it or not, but when the observations of two figures on the opposite ends of the political spectrum converge, chances are that they are onto something.

In closing, let me turn to a Canadian scholar's highly imaginative and insightful critique of Huntington's *Clash*. Michael Keren (2008) employs Yann Martel's classic, *Life of Pi* (2001), as a metaphor to repudiate three of Huntington's basic assumptions: that religious revival contradicts scientific rationality, that civilizations are mutually exclusive, and that conflict between civilizations is imminent. Pi regards religion and science as complementary guides for the fulfilment of human life, and although he was a Hindu by birth, he evolved into a syncretist, uniting the traditions of Hinduism, Christianity, and Islam. Like Huntington, Keren too evokes Pearson's insight that civilizations have superseded nations as the cornerstone of international relations, but then he states that peaceful coexistence with other civilizations has become a pillar in Canadian foreign policy; this is a curious claim for an article published in 2008 when Stephen Harper was already dividing the nations of the world into friends and foes. More satisfying by far is Keren's suggestion that Martel's worldly perspective reflects his upbringing in multicultural Canada.

part three

The Canadian Dream

chapter six

Gender, Aboriginals, and Resistance

This chapter has three aims: to examine the record of Canadian women and Aboriginals in the First and Second World Wars, to consider the impact of the Harper government on these two key constituencies, and to reflect more generally on inequality's quarrelsome progeny: oppression and resistance.

Gender and War

In recent decades a huge contradiction has emerged in and challenged the feminist movement (Jones 2002): how to square its historic opposition to war with the legions of women who have chalked up their own victory for gender equality by prying open the doors of the male-dominated Armed Forces?

There is, of course, nothing new about the contribution of Canadian women to the nation's wars (see Chenier 2006; Dundas and Durflinger n.d.; and Veterans Affairs Canada 2014). In the First World War more than 2800 nursing sisters from religious orders were integrated into the Canadian Army Medical Corps. During the Second World War their head count soared to about 4500; altogether, approximately 50,000 women served in the army, navy, and air force, initially in clerical positions, but eventually as drivers, mechanics, parachute riggers, code breakers, and espionage agents. The effect was to free up men for the front lines – sometimes an unwelcome outcome for those comfortably cocooned in administrative or non-combat duties.

In 1941 the Women's Division of the Royal Canadian Air Force was formed with about 17,000 members at its peak. A month later the Canadian Women's Army Corps, with around 21,000 members, was created. Within another year the navy completed the picture by establishing the 7,000-strong Women's Royal Canadian Naval Service.[1] The navy was the hardest nut to crack, possibly because of the confined quarters of a ship, and its resistance to female recruits persisted long after the war. Yet by 2007 a woman had been appointed commander of the Naval Reserve, and two years later another woman had assumed command of a warship, HMCS *Halifax* (Veterans Affairs Canada 2014).

Actually, Canada emerged as a world leader in gender equality in the armed services. By 2001 all positions were opened to women. By 2013 women composed an impressive 12 per cent of the Canadian Forces. Even earlier, in 2005, women became eligible for combat duties. Sadly, a year later in Afghanistan Nichola Goddard became the first Canadian female soldier to be killed on the battlefield (Chenier 2006).

Women who stayed home also played a significant role in the war effort. In addition to keeping the household running and making and gathering clothing and other supplies for the troops, they entered the workforce in impressive numbers, taking over clerical and factory jobs previously deemed male occupations, such as the production of munitions.

Although it requires great courage for individuals to publicly oppose their nations' wars, there were conscientious objectors such as the Quakers, and female pacifists such as Agnes Macphail (McKay and Swift 2012, 192) who in 1921 became Canada's first woman MP. A member of the pacifist Reorganized Church of Latter Day Saints, she implied that soldiers who paid the ultimate price in the First World War had died in vain, because in her view crass economic gain rather than ideals of freedom and justice was the prime motive for the war.

The clash between civilian women who opposed and supported the First World War appears to have been considerably more overt and robust in the United States (Steinson 1980). The Women's Peace Party was pacifist, opposed to the war and to their sons' involvement in it. The civilian Women's Section of the Navy League viewed the war as a noble endeavour critical for the defence of the homeland and encouraged their sons to sign up for duty. The first group thought war was avoidable. The second group believed that war was inevitable and urged the nation to be prepared for the worst. Steinson argued that the war experience of these women fostered subsequent feminist aspirations and not just in the Women's Peace Party. Both groups emerged from the war years with increased self-esteem and sentiments of sisterhood, qualities that were reinforced during the Second World War.

It has long been recognized that the Second World War had a profound impact on both the colonial world and women's quest for equality. Colonial subjects who fought on the battlefields of Europe and elsewhere carried visions of their own liberty with them when they returned home. In 1948 India gained its independence, and by the mid-1960s the colonial world had essentially collapsed.

Progress for women initially appeared to be less certain. The main motives of women who had joined the Canadian Forces were similar to men's: patriotism and adventure. In due time they also valued the camaraderie of military life, and although they were paid less than men of the same rank doing the same job, many of them wanted to remain in the services. That was not to be. In 1946 their units were disbanded. Women at home experienced a similar fate. Those who occupied positions in the federal government were required by law to resign at the end of the war, and women employed in other jobs were expected to return to the kitchen. The implication is that the massive entry of women into the paid workforce was a necessary but temporary measure that had run its course (Chenier 2006). Yet by the 1960s the burgeoning feminist movement had captured the attention of much of the nation, whether one applauded or condemned it.

It would be an exaggeration to claim that the two world wars were the sole, or even the single most important, source of the revolution in gender relations. Even before the end of the nineteenth century, women's suffrage was a growing political force. In 1893 the National Council of Women of Canada was established (Anderson 2006). In that era some women worked outside the home, but they were mostly young and unmarried or from families without a male breadwinner. Even then the National Council of Women had agitated for equal pay for equal work. By 1918 women were granted (or won) the right to vote federally; four years later they became eligible to vote in all provincial elections except in Quebec. In 1967 a Royal Commission on the Status of Women was established, out of which emerged a lobby group, the National Action Committee, and a portfolio for the Status of Women in the federal Cabinet. While these gains in gender equality had multiple sources, an influential one probably was the experience of women both abroad and at home in previous male domains during the two world wars.

Gender and the Harper Government

In the run-up to the 2015 federal election, plans were made (Kingston 2015) for an all-party meeting on women's issues labelled "Up for Debate." Harper ducked the engagement, pleading prior commitments. As an alternative, a decision was made to interview party leaders singly. Once again the former prime minister declined to participate.

How to explain? Possibly Harper thought it was divisive to focus solely on women, and no doubt he was aware of the polls that showed (McKay and Swift 2012, 21) that women were much less supportive than men for the single foreign policy initiative that defined his tenure as prime minister: the Afghanistan adventure. His political instincts might also have warned him that the debate might unfairly deteriorate into a feminist rant against his right-wing agenda – unfairly, because in his perspective his policies were the key to fashioning a nation in which all citizens benefited, women included. Let us examine the record.

The Liberal government under Paul Martin's leadership had been poised to introduce a national childcare program. After the Conservatives were elected, the program was scrapped (Dobbin 2010). Yet the need for family support was obvious, if only for the optics; as Hamandi (2015) reported, UNICEF had ranked Canada at the bottom among twenty-five developed nations regarding early childhood education and care. The eventual response of the Conservatives was to provide all young families, regardless of income, with a taxable monthly income of $100, a paltry sum in view of the cost of a respectable childcare facility. Actually, the stipend was a step in the correct direction, because when the Family Allowance, introduced in 1945, was cancelled in 1992, Canada became the only industrial nation without a child tax concession or family allowance.

Status of Women Canada came under the baleful scrutiny of the Conservatives. Its funding was decimated, forcing twelve of its sixteen offices across the country to close their doors. The $1 million annual grant to the organization for research projects also was eliminated (Dobbin 2010). Women had been prominent among those who had relied on the Court Challenges Program that promoted human rights; it suffered the same fate. More than three dozen women's organizations, including shelters, lost their funding. Then there was the Liberal initiative to establish pay equity for women. The Conservatives dumped it too. Before Harper became prime minister, Canada had ranked seventh in the world in the gender pay gap. By 2009 it had fallen to twenty-fifth.

Conservative ideology also intruded into gender issues abroad. The Harper government eliminated a human rights agency that supported women's health, training and counselling in seventeen countries. While Harper was careful to avoid any debate about the volatile issue of abortion in Parliament, his government refused to fund clinics in developing countries that performed abortions. And at home the Conservatives threatened to deny charitable status to organizations or groups that lobbied for human rights – unless their goals coincided with the government's ideology.

Given the Conservative government's record, it is difficult to disagree with Nadeau (2011, 104–5) that women bore the brunt of the budget cuts. This does not mean, however, that the Conservative Party was anti-women, otherwise how to explain why so many articulate and confident spokeswomen were attracted to its platform? It would be more accurate to assert that the Conservatives were anti-feminist, clearly displayed in the delight expressed by the right-wing group, Real Women, when Status of Women

Canada was hit by devastating cuts to its budget. From the perspective of the Conservatives, the apparent assault on women was
nothing of the sort. Instead it was a cleansing operation meant to
scrub away the dysfunctional liberal philosophy that prevented
women from realizing their potentials.

Although the Conservatives might contend that their mandate
expired before they had time to complete the right-wing revolution, there is little evidence of positive results for the country or
women. For example, just over two decades ago, in 1994, Canada
was ranked (Hamandi 2015) at the top on both the UN's Human
Development Index and gender equality measures. Towards the
end of Harper's reign, the country had fallen to eighth and twenty-
third place respectively.

Ironically, even a leaked report prepared by Status of Women
Canada during Harper's time in office (Beeby 2015) revealed that in
terms of gender equality Canada had dropped behind other developed nations. Poverty rates for elderly single women and women-
headed families had increased. Moreover, the country ranked near
the bottom in the gender gap for paid work and lacked a national
strategy to address violence against women. What a risky report! If
heads did not roll at Status of Women Canada, the Harper government must have already lost its touch.

Aboriginals and War

In the mid-1960s on a visit to the Commonwealth Institute in London, England, which contained a permanent exhibition representing the member nations, I was stunned by the duplicity of the
Canadian display. It was dominated by Inuit and First Nation art,
craft, and history. What a contradiction: on the one hand the portrayal of Aboriginals as the cultural soul of the country, seemingly
celebrated and privileged above all others, and on the other hand
the centuries of discrimination and desolation at home.[2]

Had the display documented the impressive contribution of the
country's Aboriginal population to the First and Second World
Wars, it would have been more genuine and less paternalistic. A

few words on terminology are in order before turning to that contribution. Historically a distinction has been made between First Nations, Inuit, and Metis. First Nations, in turn, were divided into non-status and status (or registered or treaty) people. The Indian Act of 1876 applied only to status First Nations. This changed in 1982 when the Constitution Act declared that the term *Aboriginal* embraces not only Inuit and Metis, but also both status and non-status First Nations (Hedican 2013, 13). Although I shall generally follow the lead of the Constitution Act and adopt the term *Aboriginal, First Nations* is often the more appropriate term in the context of the two world wars. This is because the Canadian government only counted status Indians who participated.

From the early days of colonialism, Aboriginals were dragged into the French-English rivalry, with the Hurons siding with the French and the Iroquois with the British. In the War of 1812 Aboriginals fought alongside British and Canadian troops, and some of them joined a small contingent of Canadian volunteers to support British soldiers in the South African Boer War of 1899 (CBC News Online 2006). It was during the First World War, however, that Canada's Aboriginals made their mark.

From the outset of the war, controversy surrounded the participation of First Nation individuals, even those with legal status under the Indian Act. Some of the opposition (National Defence 2010) was based on prejudice: the "natives" were not considered proper material to serve the nation in its time of need. Other opposition was more benevolent: the view that it was unfair to expect status Indians to fight in the war because they did not enjoy the full rights and privileges of citizens. They were not allowed to vote, and there were restrictions on cultural practices such as the potlatch, wearing traditional dress, speaking Indigenous languages, and even on travel beyond the reserves.

Then there were the objections of Aboriginals themselves. Some bands (as First Nations at the time were labelled) made their participation contingent on being recognized as sovereign nations, on a par in this respect with Canada and Great Britain. Other bands had clauses in their treaties that exempted them from obligatory military service for the state (CBC News Online 2006).

When conscription was introduced in 1917, status Indians were not exempted. By 1918, possibly because of their protests, they no longer were required by law to register for military service. They could, however, be obligated to participate in non-combat duties at home. Sometimes this simply translated into filling vacant manual labour and factory positions. For example, in one fish canning factory in British Columbia, more than 500 of the employees were Aboriginal men and women.

Aboriginal women, incidentally, also contributed to the war effort by making clothing available to the troops and even raising money for the war effort despite their shallow pockets. Just as Euro-Canadian women who had entered the paid workforce had to step aside for the returning veterans, so too did Aboriginals when the war was over (Indigenous and Northern Affairs Canada 2014).[3]

It was obvious that what status Indians objected to was obligatory military duty, because both before and after conscription a remarkable number of them – about 4000, or one-third of the eligible male age category (similar to the percentage of Euro-Canadian soldiers) – served in the war. Like Canadian men in general, their motives included patriotism and adventure, plus the attraction of a guaranteed wage, respect for the British Crown, and, possibly, a warrior tradition embedded in their cultures.

The vast majority of these First Nation volunteers enlisted in the army. Sometimes stereotyped by the military command, and occasionally demonstrating actual expertise in hunting and bush lore, many of them were assigned as snipers and scouts. Language barriers and unfamiliarity with mainstream Canadian culture in addition to the rules-oriented, hierarchical character of the military often made adjustment a challenge for the recruits. As testimony to their success in meeting it, they accrued their share of medals for valour, and along the way an unanticipated benefit of the war experience blossomed. Stereotypes in the barracks and trenches about the country's Indigenous population faded away, and a sense of mutual respect and camaraderie emerged as Natives and non-Natives got to know each other as individuals.

More than 300 status First Nation soldiers died in the Great War, either in combat or as a result of diseases such as tuberculosis, which sometimes were carried back to the reserves with devastating consequences. At the conclusion of the war, funds were made available to veterans for the purchase of land and farming equipment. First Nation veterans discovered that they were excluded from the program, possibly because land on reserves is a collective rather than individual resource. They also woke up at home to the reality that virtually nothing had changed in their rights and privileges in Canada. They were still wards of the state, still denied the freedoms that Euro-Canadians enjoyed, and still enmeshed in poverty and subjected to the prejudice and discrimination that had marked their lives before the war.

Even during the final years of the First World War, the Canadian government had acted in bad faith towards First Nations. In order to increase food production, "idle" land on reserves (Indigenous and Northern Affairs Canada 2014) – land not being farmed – was taken over by the government and made available to non-Natives. This was contrary to the Indian Act, which stated that reserve land could not be expropriated without the consent of reserve members. The government's reaction was to amend the Indian Act in 1918 so that consent was no longer required. The land involved was not returned to the control of the reserves until four years after the war ended.

The response of some Aboriginal veterans was to turn to political activity. Lieutenant F.O. Loft, a Six Nations member, established the country's first pan-Aboriginal political organization, the League of Indians of Canada. A decade later, in 1927, the Indian Act was again revised, this time to ban all native political organizations beyond the local band level (Hedican 2013, 26) and to make it illegal for Aboriginals to hire lawyers in support of their political aspirations (Saul 2014, 73).

As far as Canada's Aboriginal population is concerned, the Second World War was essentially a rerun of the Great War. Once again only status First Nation recruits were officially counted, although they were reinforced by some Inuit and numerous Metis volunteers. Conscription, introduced in 1942, proved just as unpopular among First Nation communities as it had in the earlier war. Altogether about 3000 men with official Indian status volunteered for the Canadian services. Neither in the First nor Second World Wars did they form a separate combat unit, although they were concentrated in a couple of battalions. Because of their low educational qualifications, few of them became regular officers, but some became non-commissioned officers such as corporals and sergeants (National Defence 2010). Education was one of the reasons why most First Nation volunteers ended up in the Infantry. A quite different reason was the informal racial criteria for recruits in the navy and air force; only a person of pure European descent was deemed acceptable (ibid. 2010).

What was different in the Second World War was the sharp increase in the number of First Nation women who volunteered as nurses. While a few may have served during the First World War, approximately seventy-two of them saw duty overseas in the women's branches of the army, navy, and air force during the Second World War.

The mortality count for Aboriginal combatants in the Second World War was more than 200, a figure that might be twice that high if non-status First Nation, Metis, and Inuit soldiers had been officially recognized. When the war was over, it was, as Yogi Berra put it, déjà vu all over again: Third World conditions in Aboriginal communities, the heavy hand of Indian agents as they applied the discriminatory regulations of the Indian Act, and of course the continuing legal status of wards of the state. There were, nevertheless, signs of change. Status Indians were granted the right to vote provincially in the 1950s, and the same privilege federally in 1960. By 2000 all Aboriginals in the Canadian Forces were officially counted, amounting that year to 1,275 individuals, or 1.4 per cent of the total number of troops. Just a year later, in 2001, the National Aboriginal Veterans War Monument was unveiled in Ottawa (CBC News Online 2006).

Aboriginals and the Harper Government

In 2005 Paul Martin almost accomplished what no previous prime minister had been able to do, including his Liberal predecessors Pierre Trudeau and Jean Chrétien: a critical breakthrough in the relations between Aboriginals and the federal and provincial governments. After eighteen months of consultations by government representatives and leaders of national Aboriginal organizations, a key meeting was held at Kelowna, British Columbia. The aim was to put together a plan that would close the socio-economic gap between Aboriginal and non-Aboriginal society. Five billion dollars over a period of five years was earmarked for Aboriginal education, housing, clean water, health services, administrative training, and economic development.

Prominent Aboriginal leaders such as Assembly of First Nations Chief Phil Fontaine were enthusiastic supporters of what became known as the Kelowna Accord (Marshall 2013), but its destiny fell into the hands of the Conservatives after they captured the Prime Minister's Office in 2006. During the next two years as the new government quibbled about the details of the accord, the writing was on the wall: the Conservatives wanted to bury it. Probably to the surprise of few observers, by 2008 it had sunk into oblivion.

The Conservatives' treatment of the Kelowna Accord set the tone for their relations with Aboriginal people. Over the years there had been disturbing rumours but few hard facts about the number of Aboriginal women who had mysteriously disappeared. Then in 2010 the Native Women's Association of Canada revealed the findings of its research – at least 600 Indigenous women and girls had been murdered or gone missing (Palmater 2015). The response of the Harper government was to cut off the organization's funding, possibly because it was sceptical of the findings. Yet a subsequent RCMP inquiry found that the number of murdered or missing women actually was closer to 1200.

Calls for a national inquiry into the tragedy were ignored by the Conservatives. Harper frankly admitted that the "issue" was not high on his party's radar and dismissed it as a law-and-order problem or crime, not a societal problem with deep roots that had to be exposed by a formal inquiry. Most of the cases, he added, had previously been solved by the police (Bronskill and Tutton 2015); after pointing out that some forty studies pertaining to the missing women already existed, the prime minister concluded that the last thing needed was yet another study. No doubt he was correct if its destiny were to gather dust like the rest of them.

Harper was not a professional economist, but he did complete a master's degree in that discipline, which makes it surprising that he put most of his eggs in one basket in terms of the economy. His single-minded obsession with the oil industry, specifically the controversial tar sands of Alberta (Nikiforuk 2010), goes a long way to explain his dismissal of Supreme Court decisions that got in the way and his legislative changes that removed barriers to resource extraction.

Some Supreme Court judges over the years have proven to be remarkably immune to government pressure. Consider, for example, the Comprehensive Land Claims Policy – federal legislation for settling claims over lands never covered by treaties (Mann 2014). The Conservative government drooled at the prospect of gaining control of these lands, and no doubt its ideology persuaded it that private ownership was in the best interests of the Aboriginals themselves. Yet the government got little help from the judicial system. For example, in a landmark decision, the Supreme Court ruled that the Tsilhgot'in Nation in British Columbia had full title to its territorial lands, and only with its consent and fair financial compensation could development projects proceed; moreover, the government could not enact legislation affecting the rights of Aboriginals without their express consent. The reaction of the Conservatives was to revise the government's Aboriginal policy in a manner that increased the pressure to convert Aboriginal territory into private property, thus undermining the Supreme Court's decision (ibid.).

Even when treaties existed, there were enormous problems. Language barriers obfuscated both oral and written communication. It seems that while First Nation people thought they were signing peace agreements, the government of the day interpreted their signatures as evidence that they were relinquishing their rights and virtually all of their lands, and accepting as compensation the splendid benefits that would flow from becoming wards of the state. Often the final version of treaties distorted what Indigenous people had thought had been agreed on verbally. In this context it is remarkable that judges have recently been willing to accept oral history as a basis for their decisions about Aboriginal land claims. As any anthropologist knows, oral history, along with myths, is the archive for people without written records.

The Harper government's early hopes for the success of the Alberta oil industry were tied to two giant companies, TransCanada's Keystone XL and Enbridge's Northern Gateway. The former's pipeline was to pass through the United States to its refineries. The latter's was to cross British Columbia to the Pacific coast. When President Obama in 2011 decided to delay the approval of Keystone XL, the Canadian government shifted its focus to Northern Gateway, sparking off massive protest from both Aboriginals and residents of all stripes in Alberta and British Columbia and even across the country.

Unfazed, the Conservative government in 2012 and 2014 enacted a series of pro-pipeline laws that accelerated the National Energy Board's environmental assessment process, enabled tax authorities to audit charities opposed to the pipelines, labelled individuals and groups in favour of environmental protection as radicals and security risks subject to RCMP and CSIS scrutiny, greatly reduced the number of waterways that had been off-limits to development projects, and revised the Indian Act to encourage the leasing of land on reserves (see Pyrstupa 2015; Palmater 2015).

Let me elaborate on the last two legislative changes. In 1882 the Navigable Waters Protection Act (NWPA) had been enacted to require a rigorous vetting process in order to prevent proposed construction projects from interfering with the traffic on waterways. The Harper government replaced the NWPA with the less demanding Navigation Protection Act. There is no mystery why the government took this step. Many of the waterways flowed through Aboriginal territory. An unintended consequence of the 1882 legislation had been to provide protection to the Canadian environment for future generations. With one stroke of the pen, the Conservatives had greatly compromised a barrier to oil, mineral, and forest exploitation and disarmed the Aboriginal communities that stood in the way.

An argument could be made that the original waterways protection act has been rendered obsolete by the passage of time and that the new legislation has the benefit of shifting responsibility from the central government to the local community, where people are more in tune with their environmental and economic needs. Similar defences, or rationalization, no doubt could be marshalled for the lease of reserve lands, especially the argument that some individuals on reserves want not only that option but also the adoption of private ownership of their property. Although a central tenet of Aboriginal culture is that land is a communal good that cannot be alienated, we should not be astounded to discover that some individuals embrace a different perspective. Aboriginals are no more homogeneous than English Canadians, French Canadians, or any other identifiable group in the country. Several years ago I came across an African Canadian who had joined a splinter Ku Klux Klan organization in Calgary, a rather bizarre example of the lack of uniformity in group thought and behaviour. Therefore, when outsiders who crave access to and control over reserve lands manage to identify a minority of individuals who favour leasing and personal ownership, we should be neither surprised nor impressed.

In 2008, the year that the Truth and Reconciliation Commission was established, Prime Minister Harper apologized to the country's Aboriginals for the residential schools that damaged so many young people and their families, and for the assault on their cultures and languages. At the same time he expressed sympathy and understanding for the determination of Aboriginals to avoid assimilation (Hedican 2013, 40–1). Despite all that has been revealed about his party's negative attitudes towards and impact on Aboriginal communities, should Harper actually be considered an ally?

Well, just a year earlier his government had refused to sign the UN Declaration on the Rights of Indigenous Peoples.[4] Shortly after the 2008 apology, he reduced the funds available for Indigenous languages (Palmater 2015). And the residential school horror notwithstanding, he has not hesitated to declare that colonialism never took root in Canada. As for assimilation, that would appear to be his top priority regarding Aboriginal people. Perhaps I'm naive, but I cannot help adding that one of the Conservative government's least generous acts was to attempt to deflect criticism from its harsh treatment of Aboriginals by broadcasting the avarice and irresponsibility of a handful of chiefs, as if they represented the vast majority of Indigenous leaders.

One of the most devastating attacks on the record of the Harper government has been levelled by Pamela Palmater (2015), a Mi'kmaw from Eel River Bar First Nation in New Brunswick, who is a professor at Ryerson University. She describes the Harper government as one of the most racist administrations in generations and states that it has destroyed what progress earlier was made in relation with First Nations. Her charge against the Harperites goes much further than pointing out that they have done little to alleviate the problems facing First Nations such as child poverty and the numbers of children in foster care and adults in prison – conditions that the UN in 2014 described as a crisis. Her most powerful accusation is that the Harper government has deliberately made life on reserves so hopeless and distressful that people have been forced to abandon their communities and start over again elsewhere. What a clever way to gain possession of Aboriginal lands and advance the goal of assimilation.

The 2015 federal election was not business as usual. The apathy and low voter turnout that has come to mark recent elections was overwhelmed by a swell of opposition to the Harper government. First Nation people were swept along by the movement. Chiefs across the country not only encouraged their people to vote, but more pointedly to cast their ballots against the Conservatives (Galloway 2015).

The chiefs were facing an uphill battle, because voter turnout in Aboriginal communities generally has been even lower than in the rest of the country. One reason no doubt was the sense of alienation from the political process. In addition, for some people the act of voting amounted to a betrayal of the long-embraced dream of achieving the status of a nation on a par with the Canadian state (Galloway 2015). Whatever the reason, the low turnout coupled to the small numbers – Aboriginals until recently formed only about 2 per cent of the country's population – meant that past federal and provincial governments could afford to trample on their rights, or at least to ignore them. For the Conservatives there was a further disincentive to court First Nation people; when they did vote they usually supported the rival political parties (Cutland 2015).

In a presumably tongue-in-cheek piece, McSheffrey (2015) actually thanked Prime Minister Harper for his harsh and disrespectful treatment of Aboriginal society, because in her view that was one of the two main factors that had begun to generate sympathy across Canada for Aboriginal people. The other was the growing appreciation for the environmental stewardship provided by First Nations, Metis, and Inuit. Central to their world view is the belief that land is a gift from the gods to be nourished rather than a commodity to be exploited. Then there is their Indigenous knowledge that informs humans how to coexist with the environment. Little wonder (Palmater 2015) that prominent figures such as Pope Francis and Canada's David Suzuki have nominated Aboriginals as the potential saviours of the planet.

Finally, some implications of the genetic and cultural frameworks. Both women and Aboriginals historically were the Other – "them" as distinct from "us" in a European-origin male-dominated universe. Rather than being a pristine biological construct, the survival of the fittest was culturalized by a masculine and ethnic discourse that dictated how women and Aboriginals were represented. The feminist movement was a cultural one too, because it revolved around gender, which is an ideological rather than a biological concept. The willing response of women to the challenges of war no doubt reflected their identification with the Canadian nation and Western civilization. The apparently similar identification among First Nations, signalled by their valiant participation in the two world wars, was all the more remarkable in view of the history of oppression; given Huntington's rambling about cleft states and the virus of multiculturalism, it is difficult to know whether he would be impressed or astounded by the Aboriginal example. Of course, the war activity of women and Aboriginals challenged the prejudice that they were not fully developed citizens and human beings and constituted one example of the myriad forms of resistance to which I now turn.

Resistance

At a teach-in held at Saskatoon in November 2012, three First Nations women and a non-Native ally sowed the seeds for a remarkable social movement to which they gave the name "Idle No More." Following the May 2011 federal election, the victorious Conservatives had tabled omnibus Bill C-45, which, among other things, compromised environmental protection and made it easier for reserve land to be leased. The teach-in was the forum these women used to register their protest.

Thousands of people, and not just Aboriginals, must have been waiting for something like Idle No More, because within days, with the help of social media such as Facebook, it had inspired "flash mobs" consisting of largely spontaneous gatherings and round dances at malls and public venues. These protest dances quickly spread from Saskatchewan to the other Western provinces and eventually across the country. Soon there were Idle No More protests in several locations in the United States and solidarity gatherings in Europe and even in New Zealand and Egypt (CBC News Online 2013). One observer, Niigaan Sinclair (2014), a professor at the University of Manitoba, described Idle No More as the largest social movement in Canada since the civil rights protests in the 1960s.

Something else occurred in late 2012 that penetrated the consciousness (and maybe the conscience) of Canadians. Theresa Spence, chief of the Attawapiskat First Nation in northern Ontario, began a forty-three-day liquid diet hunger strike to prod Prime Minister Harper and Governor-General David Johnston to meet with her about the atrocious living conditions on reserves, her own included. Chief Spence's sacrifice added further inspiration to the supporters of the Idle No More movement (CBC News Online 2013).

Idle No More is a grassroots initiative with no formal ties to any political party or organization, including the Assembly of First Nations. Normally the leader of the AFN is constrained to remain impartial regarding party politics and to walk gingerly around controversial issues. However, roles are elastic, and each incumbent decides whether or not and how far to stretch them. Shawn Atleo, the AFN chief at the time, was measured in his public comments. He expressed his support for Idle No More and took advantage of its popularity to nudge government officials towards the bargaining table.

Although it is probably too soon to comment on the long-range prospects of Idle No More, there is a question that can be reasonably raised right now: how can its early impressive growth and widespread impact be explained? There are, I think, two key reasons. First, the Harper government had turned the heat up in its relations with First Nations until it had reached the boiling point. Second, Idle No More from the outset was dedicated to non-violent protest. This feature, along with the fact that it had been launched by women, reflecting their historic prominence in Aboriginal society, may have made the movement palatable to bystanders; it may also have rendered it a more ambiguous and slippery target than warriors manning the barricades for the state's specialists in order and control, namely the police and the courts.

The potential payoff of opting for non-violent rather than violent protest may be reflected in the case of Nunavut. In 1999 it became Canada's newest self-governing region, an enormous homeland carved out of the Northwest Territories for the primarily Inuit population. Hedican (2013, 34–6), an expert on Canada's Aboriginals, makes much of the Inuit's aversion to confrontation and preference for dialogue as an explanation for their successful negotiations with the Canadian government.

Non-violence may well have been a factor, but in my judgment it possibly was overshadowed by two other influences mentioned by Hedican. One was communication. There are over fifty languages in addition to numerous dialects spoken among First Nations, while only a single Indigenous language, Inuktitut, is spoken by the Inuit. The other factor is the benefit of geographical isolation. The Inuit largely escaped colonial administration, diseases such as smallpox, and the residential school system. At the same time they retained their language, cultural heritage, and to some degree their traditional lifestyle. Many years ago Frank (1970) focused on the development of underdevelopment in Third World nations. His argument was that the less their contact with developed nations, the greater their social and economic viability. The Inuit case is a variation on Frank's thesis.

Cynical though it may seem, my guess is that Nunavut, with its isolation and small population (about 25,000 in 1999), came into being partly because it was a politically inexpensive way for the Canadian government to display to the world its benevolence towards Indigenous peoples.

If the average Canadian thinks about Aboriginal protests, it is probably the image of violence rather than non-violence that surfaces. Yet what astounds me, in view of the provocation aimed at Aboriginals and the injustice they have borne, is just how rarely violence has erupted. Most protests have consisted of marches in public and gatherings outside the Parliament buildings in Ottawa and the provinces. Even the protesters' preferred tactic, erecting barricades at highways, bridges, and rail lines, is essentially an inconvenience to the public rather than a threat to lives. The usual pattern in violent protest is to begin by attacking property and then up the ante by targeting persons. In Canada only occasionally has Aboriginal protest even reached the first stage.

This brings us to two of the most dramatic cases of violent protest in recent decades: Oka and Ipperwash (see Hedican 2013). The Oka confrontation in Quebec was ignited by what must have appeared to outsiders as a rather mundane dispute about a golf course.

In 1989 the town council of Oka gave developers a green light to expand the local golf course from nine to eighteen holes and to construct sixty luxury condos. By doing so the council enflamed deep resentment among Mohawks on two nearby reserves, the Kahnawake and Kanehsatake Nations, who had been petitioning to be recognized as the legal owners of the land slated for development as far back as the early 1700s.

From the Mohawk perspective, the nine-hole golf course, which was built in 1961 and bordered a burial ground, was illegal. The proposed expansion of the course would have swallowed the burial ground, and the condo complex would have been a fait accompli further complicating the Mohawk cause.

When the Mohawks blocked access to the disputed land in 1990, the mayor of Oka summoned the Quebec Provincial Police (the Sûreté du Québec). A violent confrontation broke out, during which a young officer, Corporal Marcel Lemay, was killed by an unidentified participant. The RCMP replaced the Sûreté, but more violent clashes with the protesters forced its withdrawal too. Then at Premier Robert Bourassa's request the army arrived. That marked the beginning of the end to the confrontation. Despite the volatile situation, no gunfire was exchanged between the Mohawk warriors and the federal troops. Eventually the protesters dismantled their blockades at the golf course, as well as one they had erected at the heavily travelled Mercer Bridge, and drifted back to their reserves.[5]

The Oka case exposes a flaw in my analysis that probably has been detected by alert readers: the focus almost entirely on the federal government's role in emasculating the lives of the country's Aboriginals. The case of Ipperwash, like that of Oka, drives home the point that provincial governments have often been equally culpable. Similar to my coverage of Oka, I shall only sketch out the bare bones of the Ipperwash confrontation. Its background is a familiar one in Aboriginal circles. In 1827 the Anishinabe residents of Sarnia, Walpole Island, Kettle Point, and Stony Point ceded 99 per cent of their territory (two million acres) to the British Crown in the Huron Tract Treaty. In 1919 the Kettle and Stony Point reserves split off from the other two. During the following decade two different real estate developers managed, with the assistance of the Indian agent, to gain ownership of some of the Stony Point reserve's beachfront property and flog it to outsiders as a recreational paradise. In 1936 the government converted this property and chunks of reserve land that bordered it into Ipperwash Provincial Park.

The park may have seemed to the Anishinabe to be the last straw, especially because there was a burial ground within its boundaries, but in 1942 under the War Measures Act some of the reserve land was expropriated for a military base. This forced Stony Point residents to move onto Kettle Point property. The understanding was that the land would be returned to the reserve when the war was over. More than fifty years later it still was in the hands of the Canadian military.

After repeated appeals over the decades to the Department of National Defence were ignored, in 1993 Stony Point members finally invaded the military camp. In 1995, following several confrontations, the military withdrew completely from what was known as Camp Ipperwash. That might have been the end of the story had someone other than Mike Harris been premier of Ontario at the time. As an official inquiry (Linden 2007) into the Ipperwash Crisis revealed, Harris appeared to be incensed with the sheer gall of "the uppity natives" (racist epithets blistered the corridors of power) and determined to unleash the full force of the OPP to crush the occupation. The tragic consequence is well known. In September 1995 a Stony Point resident, Dudley George, was shot and killed by an OPP officer, Ken Deane.[6]

What do the Oka and Ipperwash crises tell us about the costs and benefits of violent protest? After the barricades around Oka were dismantled, several protesters were arrested, but only a couple of them received prison sentences. The plans for the golf course expansion and luxury condos were shelved, and a decade later the federal government granted the Mohawks legal ownership of almost 1000 hectares.

The formal Ipperwash Inquiry concluded that Deane had been aware that George was unarmed; the officer was eventually convicted of criminal negligence and sentenced to 180 hours of community service. In 2006 he died in a car accident. In 2003 the family of Dudley George won a civil suit against former premier Harris and several members of his Cabinet and was awarded a settlement from the OPP. Earlier, in 1998, each member of the Kettle and Stony Point Nations received a sizeable land claim settlement. With the former military base already in their possession, all that remained in order to restore the integrity of the territory to which they had rights by the treaty of 1827 was Ipperwash Provincial Park. In 2009 the Ontario government formally ceded ownership and control of the park to the Stony Point and Kettle Point Nations.

It would seem, then, that the violent protests in both Oka and Ipperwash paid dividends, but the price tag was considerable. In each setting a human being ended up dead, and no doubt lingering bitterness on all sides soured their subsequent interaction. For those who embrace non-violent protest, not only was the price too high, but it also was not the sole option, as illustrated by Idle No More and Nunavut. For others, without violence or at least its threat, nothing can be accomplished. As the saying goes, only the squeaky wheel gets the grease. In an authoritative article on the Oka confrontation, Zig Zag (2014) not only accepted that adage as a truism borne out by the Oka experience but also observed that the militant response of the Mohawks set the tone and style for Aboriginal protest for the rest of the 1990s and beyond. It might be added, with Fanon in mind ([1961] 1963), that violence can have a salutary cleansing impact on the mentality of people who have been ground into the dirt over the centuries.

My own position is that it is a mistake to portray violence and non-violence as incompatible forces. They often go hand in hand, comparable to the good cop/bad cop duet, or the reciprocal influence of soft and hard power. In this context, it could be argued that without the vivid examples of violent protest in Oka and Ipperwash in the early 1990s, Idle No More may not have been embraced so enthusiastically a few years later. The Oka and Ipperwash confrontations may even have influenced the Canadian government's decision to give its blessing to Nunavut.

A few final thoughts regarding resistance. What surprises me about Oka and Ipperwash is that the body count was so low. What astounds me about resistance in general, whether violent or non-violent, is that it sometimes works. If resistance is the weapon of the weak, as Scott put it (1985), oppression is the weapon of the strong. Both weapons are the polarized products of institutionalized inequality, but they differ drastically in firepower, tactics, and goals.

The ruling class enjoys a monopoly over both hard and soft power. It controls the instruments of force, and its interests are represented in the reigning ideology. In contrast, protesters such as those in Oka and Ipperwash have two strikes against them from the outset. Not only are they outgunned, but they also are portrayed as barbarians at the gates, threats to the orderly society. There normally is a bias in favour of order in most societies. Order connotes legitimacy. When a scattering of protesters mobilize and challenge the status quo, not only the ruling class but also the vast bulk of the citizenry are inclined to dismiss their causes as illegitimate.

When society is humming along smoothly like a well-oiled engine, social control is usually subtle and inconspicuous; ideology and manipulation take care of business. But when the gears begin to grind, the ruling class must spring into action, and in this situation more often than not it mobilizes its specialty: the pre-emptive strike. The resisters possess their own overt specialty: guerrilla warfare. However, many forms of resistance tend to be covert and indirect. A widespread tactic among people who are oppressed is to conceal part of themselves from public view. Many years ago on a trip to Sudan in East Africa, I met some American businessmen who arranged for one of their local employees to act as my guide. In the company of the businessmen, he was genial and almost obsequious, loyal to the bone. Yet when we set off to fish in the Red Sea, his demeanour was transformed. It turned out that he was a committed Marxist, well-read, and fuelled with nationalist fervour. He despised the Americans and lumped me in with them. Never shall I forget his repeated question: what had I done to the "red Indians" of Canada?

A more controversial example of covert and indirect resistance has been suggested by Riches (1986, 15–20). In his view excessive alcoholic consumption among the Inuit is actually a political statement; it is the Inuit way of rejecting the values and authority of mainstream Canadian society. Of course, Euro-Canadians in the Arctic are all teetotallers.

A third example, no doubt equally controversial, touches on the tragedy of suicide. In parts of Papua New Guinea, suicide has been portrayed (Berndt 1962; Counts 1991; and Stewart and Strathern 2002) as a variant on the act of resistance. Some individuals who have been shamed exact revenge by taking their own lives. Although humiliation no doubt has been a prevalent emotion among Canadian Aboriginals, I lack the expertise to comment on whether or not it has been a factor in their horrendous suicide rate, especially among young people.

Earlier I expressed puzzlement, in view of the advantages enjoyed by the ruling class, about how resistance sometimes manages to be effective. The challenge for the oppressor is much less than for the oppressed. The former only has to maintain the status quo to emerge victorious. The latter has to effect a change in society's institutional framework. The key element in resistance, I think, is a motive that is ubiquitous among human beings but especially prominent among the marginalized. There is a name for this powerful motive. It is called revenge.

Lessons Learned

There are at least two significant lessons to be learned from the participation of women and Aboriginals in the First and Second World Wars. One is that there is no basis for the adage that women are naturally opposed to war. The other is that there is no guarantee that the sacrifice of veterans will translate into improved living conditions and opportunities for them back home.

The involvement of women in war has deep roots. As Turney-High has commented in reference to hunting and gathering societies ([1949] 1971, 152), "The opinion that women inherently hate war is not borne out by the facts." In such societies, he added, it was often the women who pressured the men to take up arms. Shaw and Wong (1989, 179–80) have argued that the human propensity for warfare is just as prevalent among women as among men. In early human history, they observed, men did most of the fighting because brute strength was then an asset, but women were the principal defenders of the home and reproduction and thus of a group's inclusive fitness.

Then there is the famous case of female soldiers in the West African territory of Dahomey (now called Benin) during the eighteenth and nineteenth centuries. Numbering more than 5000 at their peak, these women served as bodyguards for the king, fought courageously and fiercely as a separate unit during the era of the slave trade wars, and helped make Dahomey the region's strongest military power (Goldstein 2001; Dash 2011). Only when French troops finally defeated Dahomey at the end of the nineteenth century and turned it into a protectorate was the Amazon corps disbanded.

Female terrorism also has deep roots. According to Knight (1979) the women who violently opposed the tsarist régime in Russia during the nineteenth century qualified as terrorists. During the 1960s and 1970s when terrorism was mainly a left-wing phenomenon, women were prominent in the Red Faction Army in Germany, the Red Brigade in Italy, and the Weather Underground in America. During the wars of colonial liberation and secessionist movements following the Second World War, women certainly were agents of violence during the Troubles in Northern Ireland and in Kenya during the Mau Mau Rebellion in the 1950s, but it was more usual for them to play a supporting role such as nursing, cooking, and providing comfort and safe havens for men.

Several years ago I investigated the vibrant independence and autonomist movement in Corsica (Barrett 1996, 193–5) and from my interviews drew several generalizations. First, although in terms of violent behaviour women were less active than men, in terms of attitudes about violence there was little difference between them; both women and men were all over the map – some enthralled by violence, others sickened by it, and another tangent bored and disinterested. Second, although women were more involved than men in peacemaking movements, this was partly because men already had claimed ownership of violence and because of cultural prejudice that associated peacemaking with women's "nature." Third, women who mobilized against violence or put economic and feminist goals ahead of nationalism were often painted as traitors, lesbians, and prostitutes; demonization went with the territory. Fourth, while most Corsican men stated that they were by nature more violent than women, they often added that women who did join one of the island's militant independence groups were inclined to be more vicious than their male comrades; some of the women who were interviewed said the same thing. Fifth, nationalist movements such as Corsica's sometimes translate into the legitimation of male dominance, the renewed validation of the patriarchal past. This partly explains why Corsican women were generally less enthusiastic than men about the prospect of independence.

In today's world terrorism has emerged as the dominant source of international strain, and women have become prominent players as suicide bombers in the Middle East and elsewhere. According to Nacos (2005), female terrorists differ little from their male counterparts in ideological commitment and brutality. What might set them apart is their motivation. Some middle-class women, Nacos suggests, gravitate to terrorism out of boredom and could be described as "women lib extremists," expressing their resistance to patriarchy in an unconventional manner. In France, which has been hit hard by terrorism, the recruitment of women from the Muslim population, including converts to Islam, has become a key element in ISIS or Daesh strategy (Rubin and Breeden 2016). Ironically, the reason why women are especially suited for terrorism is the same that allows them to excel in anthropological fieldwork. In both settings women are perceived as less threatening than men and thus more capable of drawing close to their subjects or targets.

As we approach the third decade of the twenty-first century, assaults on women and girls in Canada persist, pay equity remains elusive, and sexism still stalks the workplace. Yet thanks largely to the feminist movement, the country that women veterans returned to after the Second World War has gradually moved closer to gender equality. As for veterans from the colonies, they have witnessed ethnic strife, political turbulence, and the parasitic impact of multinational corporations. Yet their nations have been liberated from the iron bonds of colonialism. In sharp contrast, First Nation veterans found little to celebrate when they were repatriated. How to explain?

Women had two advantages over Aboriginals. First, in this context as distinct from gender, they were not "the Other." To the contrary, the lives of women and men are almost inseparable from cradle to grave. Second, rather than being a minority group in Canadian society, females actually outnumber males. As we shall see, to a considerable degree demography is destiny.

The advantage of Europe's colonies over Canadian Aboriginals turns on the distinction between classical and internal colonialism. The former can be divided into administrative and settler types. Kwame Nkrumah, the former president of Ghana and champion of pan-African nationalism, once contemplated (but never executed) a plan to erect a statue in honour of the mosquito. It was the threat of malaria and other rampant diseases that favoured the model of term-limited revolving administrators (and sometimes indirect rule) in much of West Africa. East and South Africa, with their more hospitable environments, encouraged the rule of white settlers.

The basic difference between classical and internal colonialism concerns demography. In the classical version, the colonizers always are a minority, immensely outnumbered by the Indigenous population. Memorable examples are Rhodesia, South Africa, Algeria, and Vietnam. As history has shown, when the winds of change sweep over the planet, classical colonialism crumbles. Internal colonialism is a different species. Here it is the Indigenous population that is dwarfed by the colonizers. This explains why it is so much more difficult to resist internal colonialism.

Classical colonialism thus exists when a majority is dominated by a minority. Internal colonialism exists when a minority is dominated by a majority. Well-known examples of the latter are Basques in Spain and, arguably, Corsicans in France. African Canadians and African Americans have also been labelled internal colonies, as have the Québécois. Even the Ogoni in the oil-rich Niger Delta in Nigeria, who have been persecuted by more numerous and powerful ethnic groups, could be considered victims of internal colonialism. This brings us to Canada's Aboriginal population. As Hicks (2004) has pointed out, it too has been described as a prime example of the machinations of internal colonialism. Although Aboriginals almost always end up as a minority, in my judgment they are a special case, a subtype of internal colonialism. Two critical factors separate them from the more general category. One is that they are the descendants of the Indigenous population. The other is that they have been the victims of genocide. Four centuries ago there were more than two million Aboriginals in Canada (Rae 2015). As a result of diseases such as smallpox and tuberculosis, as well as the deliberately inhumane policies of the European colonizers, their population shrank to about 100,000 souls.

As a special case of internal colonialism, Canada has much in common with the United States, Australia, and New Zealand. In all four cases Indigenous people have been the targets of genocide. Curiously, all of them were British colonies. Even more curious, they had something else in common: none of them signed the UN Declaration of the Rights of Indigenous Peoples when it was released in 2007.

It is tempting to include Japan in this list. The history of the Ainu, the Indigenous people in Japan (and less numerously in Russia), is almost identical to the four cases above (Fogerty 2008). There too diseases carried by the rapidly expanding immigrant Japanese decimated the Ainu population. As elsewhere, assimilation emerged as the policy of the times. The Ainu language was banned, their land was confiscated, they were forbidden to hunt and fish, and their families were broken up to provide labour for Japanese enterprises. From the perspective of the Japanese state, the Ainu were invisible; they simply didn't exist. Indeed, it was not until 2008 that the Ainu were formally recognized by the Japanese government as an Indigenous people.

It is useful to draw a distinction between classical genocide and cultural genocide. The first type dominated Canada's early history. In other words, the solution to the "Indian Problem" was to make it disappear by a combination of force and neglect. As the population numbers show, this policy was effective but incomplete, because pockets of Indigenous people survived. It was at this juncture that the strategy began to shift to cultural genocide in the form of assimilation, the residential school system being its signature tactic.

Many non-Aboriginal Canadians genuinely concerned about the welfare of "the natives" have promoted assimilation as the solution. Had they been more in tune with what Aboriginals thought and desired, they would have realized that assimilation has usually been regarded as a death sentence. This brings us to one of the more notorious documents in Canadian history: "The White Paper" produced in 1969 by Prime Minister Pierre Trudeau and his minister of Indian affairs, Jean Chrétien (see "The White Paper 1969"; Sinclair 2015). Their unremarkable assumption was that Aboriginal Canadians had not shared the fruits of the Just Society.[7] Their solution was to remove virtually everything that identified Aboriginals as a distinct people. The White Paper advocated abolition of both the Indian Act and the Department of Indian Affairs, the elimination of Indian status, the conversion of reserve land into private property, the gradual termination of treaties, and the transfer of responsibility for Indian affairs to the provinces (only a temporary measure, because such affairs were to be absorbed into general programs).

What is perplexing is that the White Paper was inspired by the Hawthorn Report (1966–7), one of the most extensive and significant studies ever produced about the challenges facing Canada's Indigenous population.[8] In the report, Aboriginals are described as citizens minus, whereas they should be citizens plus, enjoying more privileges than non-Aboriginals because of their Indigenous status. The report recommended the end of all efforts to force assimilation, especially the residential schools, and recognized the right of individuals to choose their own paths in life, just as non-Aboriginals do, including whether or not to live on reserves.

If the Harper government had released the equivalent of the White Paper, it would have been bombarded with criticism. How then did the Trudeau government misread the hopes and ambitions of Aboriginal society so grievously? It wasn't for lack of consultation, because meetings with representatives of First Nations and government officials were extensive. The simple answer, I suppose, is that ideological commitment, in this case to the ethical vision known as the Just Society, can be so overwhelming that one is rendered blind to its shortcomings.

Hedican has argued (2013, 49) that the White Paper represented a termination policy, not assimilation; in his words, it amounted to "a reversal of the previous assimilation policy." With apologies to Hedican, this makes no sense to me. In my judgment the White Paper constitutes assimilation pursued to its ultimate conclusion. In other words, logic would suggest that termination and assimilation are synonyms, not contrasting policies.

The reaction of Aboriginals to the White Paper was so quick and harsh that within a year it had been tossed into the garbage bin by our former prime minister. Leading the attack against the White Paper was a young Cree named Harold Cardinal, who, at the time, was the leader of the Indian Association of Alberta. He probably spoke for most Aboriginals when he described the White Paper as extermination through assimilation, or cultural suicide pure and simple.

After Cardinal articulated his uncompromising opposition to the White Paper in *The Unjust Society* (1969), he became a household name in Canada. He also was the principal author of "Citizens Plus" (Indian Chiefs of Alberta 2011), a document with a similar message prepared by the Indian Association of Alberta. While in his forties, he embarked on the formal study of law at the University of Saskatchewan, and then completed a master's degree in law at Harvard University. Prior to his tragic death from cancer in 2005 at the age of sixty, he had become recognized as one of the most dedicated and accomplished champions of Aboriginal people of his times. In 1999 he received an honorary doctorate in law from the University of Alberta, and in 2005 another honorary doctorate from the University of British Columbia.

In recent decades some dramatic changes have taken place in Aboriginal society. Nowhere is this more evident than in relation to demography. As the fastest growing sector in the country, its population has increased to 4 per cent of the Canadian total, in the process climbing over the one million mark. Hedican (2013, 252) interprets the increase negatively, concerned that it will further dilute scarce resources. His pessimism may be warranted if the status quo prevails, but the population boost is not the only significant change taking place. As Saul (2014) has observed, Canada's Indigenous people have made a stunning comeback. There now is a host of highly educated, capable, and sophisticated Indigenous spokespeople (lawyers, judges, professors, and scientists) determined to elevate their people to a position of equality in Canada – with or without the cooperation of mainstream society.

Of course, they stand on the shoulders of past giants such as Harold Cardinal and George Manuel. Manuel, born in 1921 and a member of the Shuswap Nation in British Columbia, attended a residential school in Kamloops. Despite suffering from tuberculosis, his accomplishments over his lifetime (he died in 1989) were so significant that he was granted an honorary degree by the University of British Columbia and made an officer of the Order of Canada.

In 1972, accompanied by none other than Jean Chrétien of "White Paper" fame, Manuel travelled to New Zealand to participate in a conference on Indigenous peoples. At the time he was president of the National Indian Brotherhood in Canada, a forerunner of the Assembly of First Nations. He returned to Canada with a big idea: an international organization of Indigenous people. Thus emerged the World Council of Indigenous Peoples (WCIP). Its first conference was held in British Columbia in 1975, and that is where the organization's secretariat was located, with Manuel at the helm (Sanders 1977). Although the WCIP was impressive enough to be granted observer status at the United Nations, by 1996 it had fallen apart. This was possibly because the divided interests that often frustrate efforts to unite people in larger associations are doubly potent in cross-cultural initiatives.

Manuel's fame was not confined to WCIP. For example, in 1974 he co-authored *The Fourth World: An Indian Reality*. The term *Fourth World* had been coined to capture the essence of sub-populations in First World countries that suffered from Third World living standards (Griggs 1992). Early in this study I had striven in vain to come up with an appropriate label to describe the subtype of internal colonialism represented by Indigenous peoples under imperial conquest. The Fourth World seems to fill the bill.

Karl Marx once quipped that slavery was a great step forward in history, because captives no longer were killed. In similar fashion, it might be argued that assimilation or cultural genocide was decidedly preferable to classical genocide, because at least people were still alive. Many of my students from the developing world were turned off Marxism because of the slavery-as-progress dictum. The historical record suggests that the reaction of Aboriginal Canadians to the supposed benefit of cultural genocide or full-blown assimilation has been much the same.

Conclusion

In recent years an increased sense of urgency appears to have energized a long-sought Aboriginal goal: sovereignty. Within a year after the establishment of Idle No More, its leaders had added sovereignty to their wish list. In virtually every confrontation between

Aboriginals and the wider public, from Oka to Ipperwash, Theresa Spence's hunger protest, and the oil fields of Alberta, the cry for self-government and nationhood has shaken the complacency of big business and government.

If the goal is to achieve political and economic autonomy for each of the approximately 2000 First Nations across the land, this would be a daunting undertaking. If it were realized, it would no doubt constitute progress but only to a limited degree, because fragmentation rather than unity would still prevail.

If the goal is to unify all First Nations into a single sovereign political entity, success would translate into a bright new era for Aboriginals, but the obstacles might be even more formidable. Jeffrey Simpson (2012), a well-known journalist, has commented that First Nation communities are too small and dispersed for sovereignty of any kind to be workable. Then there is the tendency for each First Nation to zealously guard its autonomy. In this context the recent agreement in principle to settle the long-contested Algonquin land claim is instructive (Tasker 2016a; Ontario 2016). The area that is involved stretches from Ottawa to North Bay. The tentative settlement includes a cash payment of at least $300 million and entails some Crown land but not private property. About 8–10,000 Algonquins qualify as beneficiaries. From all appearances this land settlement should be celebrated by Aboriginals across the country. Yet bordering Iroquois communities condemned it as a fraud, claiming that many of those poised to benefit were not Algonquin descendants at all or had no ties to the Algonquin nation for over a century; even other Algonquin communities beyond the settlement boundaries raised similar objections (Canadian Press 2016).

The most imaginative solution to the challenge of sovereignty was the Royal Commission on Aboriginal Peoples (RCAP). Launched in 1991 as a direct response to the Oka Crisis, it was co-chaired by George Erasmus, a former chief of the Assembly of First Nations, and Justice René Dussault, a member of the Quebec Appeal Court. The final report of the RCAP (1996) covered virtually every important issue that confined Aboriginals to the situation memorably labelled by Hawthorn as "citizens minus." Noteworthy was the emphasis that the report placed on maintaining a land base for future generations. One of the boldest recommendations of the RCAP was the establishment of a special Aboriginal parliament to be known as "the House of First Peoples." The proposal entailed converting the 2000 or so First Nations into thirty to fifty larger entities whose function would be similar to that of the provinces and represent the interests of Aboriginals in relations with the federal government.

Among the many possible criticisms of the proposed House of First Peoples, such as whether the individual First Nations would agree to relinquish their autonomy and join one of the thirty to fifty larger associations, and how overall leadership would be satisfactorily arranged, perhaps the most surprising was expressed by Hedican (2013, 28–34). After correctly pointing out that the majority of Aboriginals in Canada now live in urban areas, he accused the Erasmus-Dussault Report of a systematic bias in favour of people who remain on reserves (in his own words, "The RCAP had a hidden agenda"). Although Hedican's knowledge of Aboriginal issues is vastly superior to mine, in this case I think that he misjudged the importance of maintaining a land base, which, by the way, the 2007 UN Declaration also recognized as critical for the survival of Indigenous peoples. Without a land base, the prospect of assimilation greatly increases.

I might add that the RCAP is consistent with the contemporary viewpoint that the time has come to scrap the Indian Act and the Department of Aboriginal Affairs, but *not* the reserve system. Indeed, the reserves are the building blocks for potentially expanded Aboriginal territories as chunks of land relinquished long ago by treaty and less formal agreements to the government are reclaimed; allowances would have to be made to reflect present-day realities. In the Algonquin settlement, for example, apparently nobody seriously considered adding the Parliament buildings, even though they were built on original Algonquin territory. Was it the possibility that a splinter faction might break ranks and occupy Parliament partly what motivated the federal and Ontario governments to finally agree to settle the Algonquin land claim? If so, their officials acted sensibly, although the farce that might have unfolded certainly would have been entertaining.

An analogy can be drawn between Israel and Aboriginal society. Although Israel could be criticized as the author of its own form of internal colonialism (the Palestinians), arguably responding to realistic security needs, the creation of the Israeli state in the wake of the Holocaust generated an enormous sense of dignity, pride, confidence, and liberty – not just for the citizens of Israel, but also for the Jewish Diaspora. It is not unreasonable to suggest that the House of First Peoples could have a similar impact on both those who remain on the reserves and their brethren who have become urban dwellers.

My final comment: if sovereignty on the grand scale envisioned by Erasmus and company (or at least at the autonomous community level) fails to materialize, half a century from now one of two outcomes will be probable. Either Aboriginals will still be citizens minus, their relations with the wider society as turbulent as ever, or assimilation will have triumphed. Only if the talented and increasingly determined Indigenous leadership manages to carve out a middle position (a compromise?) between sovereignty and dependency is the future likely to unfold differently.

chapter seven

Lamb Power and Tiger Power

President Obama's memorable remark when he addressed the Canadian Parliament in June 2016 – the world needs more Canada – is worthy of reflection. It is unlikely that he was making a case for greater Canadian participation in the Western alliance and its wars, because that was the preoccupation of the decade-long Harper government. More probable, Obama was recognizing and applauding the new Trudeau government's international perspective, preference for diplomacy, and sensitivity to injustice.

These, of course, were Obama's values, and opinion is divided on whether they served him well during his two terms in office. If his achievements were modest, this was largely because of the uncompromising resistance of the Republican Party and the complexity of global conflicts. He failed to shut down the holding pen for terrorists at Guantanamo Bay. Then there was ISIS. One school of thought has it that ISIS, ISIL, or Daesh was the evil progeny of George W. Bush's invasion of Iraq. Another school fingers Obama as the culprit for prematurely withdrawing American troops in 2011, creating a vacuum into which radical Muslims plunged. Judgment about Obama's strategy has been equally contested. His reluctance to flood ISIS-held territory with American ground troops because he thought that would generate a new generation of jihadists seemed wise and sound, but his critics interpreted it as Chamberlain-like appeasement, possibly even an admission that American power was slipping.

Obama also was mocked by the Republicans for ignoring the line that he had drawn in the sand in response to the Syrian state's aggression; yet with the deadly mixture of ISIS fighters and the proxy civil war between Shias and Sunnis, in addition to the Kurd equation and the dubious democratic credentials of the Syrian rebels, it was virtually impossible to separate the good guys from the bad guys.

Against the above are Obama's stunning accomplishments. First, it was his administration that negotiated the deal to terminate (at least for the time being) Iran's ambition to join the nuclear-arms club. Second, he laid the groundwork for normalizing relations between the United States and Cuba. Third, eventually his commitment to justice and equality was expressed by his public support of the LGBTQ community. Fourth, he brought America in line with the majority of nations devoted to protecting the environment from devastating climate change. Fifth, he established government-sponsored health coverage for a large chunk of Americans; it was a watered-down version of what he had aimed for, but he succeeded where every previous president had failed. Sixth, to a considerable degree the respect with which he was accorded around the globe helped to make America likeable again. Finally, and most important of all, he did not launch any new wars; under his leadership the world remained saner and safer than it might otherwise have been. In chapter 1 I implied that few outstanding statesmen have emerged since the Second World War. There have been exceptions, and leading the list in recent times is Barack Obama.

As a middle-range power, Canada does not provide its prime minister with the opportunity to make as big a splash on the world stage as does America, but Justin Trudeau's election in 2015 has not gone unnoticed. With his attractive appearance, "sunny" ways, support for suffering populations such as Syrian refugees, and for efforts to combat climate change, within a year in office he had already recaptured some of the international goodwill that the country previously had enjoyed. A change in direction that especially resonated with Canadians was the renewed commitment to peacekeeping. This commitment is more symbolic than transformational in managing conflict, but it does reinforce one of the government's early claims to the world at large: Canada is back.

On the home front, the Trudeau government reversed the previous administration's refusal to hold a public inquiry about the missing Aboriginal women (Steward 2016). Selected to lead the inquiry was Marion Butler, a Saskatchewan Cree who in 1994 became British Columbia's first Aboriginal female judge. Trudeau also committed his government to renewed efforts to close the gap between Aboriginals and the wider society, and to a nation-to-nation dialogue with the country's Indigenous population – possibly a step towards the long-sought goal of sovereignty (Bryden 2016).

Not to be overlooked is the composition of the Liberal Cabinet: fully half of the thirty members are women.

Although the Liberals enjoyed a remarkably long honeymoon, the glow surrounding any new administration must eventually fade as controversial and potentially divisive choices, often involving the economy, the military, and justice, demand action. A case in point was the government's decision to give its blessing to Site C Dam, a huge hydroelectric project on the Peace River in British Columbia that had been adamantly opposed by First Nation communities. Even more volatile was the government's decision about pipelines. Although the Northern Gateway option favoured by the previous administration was rejected, as well as Keystone XL, the green light was flashed for Kinder Morgan's Trans Mountain pipeline that would stretch from Edmonton to Burnaby in British Columbia, and for Enbridge's Line 3 that would traverse Alberta into Minnesota and Wisconsin (Tasker 2016b).

While Trudeau portrayed these decisions as critical for the country's future prosperity and emphasized that plans for implementing the most sophisticated safety measures were well advanced, as well as the carbon tax initiative, his carefully constructed image as an environmentalist took a hit. Some First Nation communities charged that they had been betrayed (Kane 2016), the mayor of Vancouver registered his protest, and so incensed was Elizabeth May, the leader of the Green Party, that she declared that she would do everything in her power to block Trans Mountain, even if she ended up in prison (Tasker 2016b). In view of these harsh reactions, reminiscent of the Conservative experience, one can only wonder if Trudeau has developed a greater sense of sympathy for his predecessor in office.

In my judgment any Canadian government has the capacity to close the economic and social gap between Aboriginals and non-Aboriginals, but to do so the Aboriginal cause must be elevated to one of its very top priorities and pursued determinably in the face of vested interests and ingrained prejudice. This requires both commitment and courage, and given the mixed (if reluctant) signals already emanating from the Liberal government, there is some doubt whether it possesses any more of these rare qualities than its predecessors, at least in relation to Indigenous issues. Little wonder that many Aboriginal leaders have concluded that the only dependable agents of change are themselves.

One of the most curious features of the twenty-first century has been the silence that has enveloped previous international efforts to ban (or at least reduce) nuclear armaments and establish protocols to remove the threat of war. It is almost as if governments everywhere had taken a long look at the massive violence that now engulfs the globe and concluded that peaceful coexistence is simply beyond the capacity of human beings. Life today seems to be driven by national interests, which, in Huntington fashion, stretch no further than to one's civilizational kin.

According to one prominent Canadian academic, Jack Granatstein (2007), the focus on interests is all to the good. Every nation, he points out, has national interests, and what is peculiar about Canada is the enormous degree to which its interests are conditioned by its relation to the United States. Because Canada depends on America for its prosperity and security, it is in its interest to do whatever it can to render its powerful neighbour benevolent. This largely explains why Granatstein thinks that Canada should have supported the ballistic missile program and the Iraq War. Although he is no fan of George W. Bush and lambastes the United States because of its woeful plans for the post-invasion era (76), as indicated earlier he believed that Iraq possessed nuclear armaments, and he supported the invasion.

Granatstein doesn't ignore the role that values play in life. Not surprisingly, being on McKay and Swift's list of new warriors, the values he admires are those intrinsic to Western civilization: freedom, openness, and democracy. He expresses support for immigration to Canada from every point on the globe, as long as new citizens have been properly vetted and are willing to embrace Canadian values. Yet he opposes multiculturalism and bluntly declares that it is a dead force in Canada (183). When to all of the above we add his distaste for the UN (especially peacekeeping) and for Quebec pacifism, it seems reasonable to conclude that our noted historian is an intellectual sibling of none other than Samuel Huntington.[1]

Lamenting the priority given to values over interests by previous administrations, especially during the Trudeau and Chrétien eras, Granatstein applauded the turn towards national interests by Martin and Harper. He also remarks that he has arrived at a new appreciation of Mulroney. No doubt this is because of Mulroney's relentless efforts to establish warm relationships with the American political elite – efforts that struck some Canadians as obsequious.

Curiously, I too have revised my previous underwhelmed impression of a former prime minister. Diefenbaker's preachiness was off-putting (apparently it churned President Kennedy's stomach), but it was his early opposition to apartheid that prepared the way for Mulroney's admirable support of Nelson Mandela. A man of his times, Diefenbaker was pro-British and pro-UN, and his anti-communism led him to support the Vietnam War. At the same time he had little love for big business and was in favour of welfare programs for the needy (Diefenbaker 1972). It was probably this progressive perspective, along with his robust nationalism, that soured his relationship with the Canadian elite and the Americans.

One of Granatstein's assertions is that it is a fantasy for Canadians to believe that they are morally superior to Americans (2007, 93). Here I am in full agreement. On one occasion in Nigeria I showed a film of a hockey game between Montreal and Toronto to my students. Their reaction was interesting: barbaric Canadians. On another occasion a newspaper vendor at the University of Ibadan in Nigeria confided that Canadians are much more decent than Americans. Hogwash!

It is the sharp difference in power and influence that sometimes creates a halo around "harmless" Canadians. A country's values, interests, and international forays are fair game for criticism, without implying that each and every citizen is complicit.

Granatstein laments the widespread anti-Americanism in Canada, labelling it sheer lunacy and a disease (2007, 205). No doubt such an attitude is counterproductive to the national interests paradigm. He also asserts that interests are permanent while values change over time, implying that the former are more important. This makes little sense to me. The values that Granatstein has identified with Western civilization presumably have been constant over the centuries, while Western interests have at one point led to military attack on a foreign power such as Japan and to overtures of friendship and cooperation at another point.

What is disturbing about Granatstein's perspective is that it seems to condone and promote unconditional support for the dominant nation regardless of the morality of its actions. The implication is that interests sometimes annihilate ethics. Furthermore, in my judgment the interests paradigm has an in-built pathological dimension: it imposes limits on international amity. Indeed, interests are a synonym for parochialism. Little wonder that so few men and women of stature, statesmen whose inspiration is unbounded, have emerged to bless us with their wisdom.

Attitudes are not stable. The passage of time and changing circumstances see to that. In a world turned upside down by terrorism and the prospect of the proliferation rather than reduction of nuclear capability, even peaceniks may look back with regret at the passing of the balance of power that deterred aggression during the Cold War. On a more parochial level, it is not beyond the realm of possibility that a Trump-like figure, exploiting the anger and fears of the diminishing white population and the struggling middle class, will shift public opinion away from the Liberals and commit the Conservative Party to the fanatical defence of Western civilization. If such a figure does capture the leadership of the Conservatives (or, much less probable, of the Liberals), Canadians of all political stripes may long for the return of Stephen Harper, who by comparison will resemble a moderate.

Does peace, then, have a chance in today's world, and what does anthropology tell us about the human potential for harmony? To answer these questions I shall present the important contributions of three anthropologists: Margaret Mead, Klaus-Friedrich Koch, and Douglas Fry. This will be followed by a brief sketch of some of the more notable mechanisms to reduce conflict that are highlighted in the ethnographic record. I shall then cast my net further and introduce the intriguing ideas of a philosopher and a playwright about how to banish war from the face of the earth.

Mead

Mead (1968, 215) defines war as "purposeful, organized and socially sanctioned combat" in which opposed groups kill each other. She adds that if a society distinguishes intra-group killing from extra-group killing, defining the first as murder but the second as legitimate, then that society supports war. Mead regards war as a social invention rather than biological instinct and recognizes that if war is to be rendered obsolete, the Us-Them dichotomy in which mutually exclusive identities and loyalties thrive, especially those now tied to the nation state, must be overcome somehow.

Mead introduces some innovative ideas about how to fashion a peaceful world, but before doing so she makes two discouraging observations. First, even if people realize that a nuclear confrontation between the great powers may well mean the wholesale destruction of human life, most of them still are willing to go to war. Second, even if somehow agreement was reached by members of the nuclear club to destroy all arsenals and ban further testing, the *knowledge* of how to construct a nuclear weapon would survive and constitute an ever-present threat to future generations.

Despite these pessimistic observations, Mead plunges on with the task of identifying alternatives to war, a task that she regards as more viable than ever, because in the nuclear age any notion that war is "functional" is indefensible.

Her starting point is to replace the nation state with nationhood. By nationhood she means a federation of interdependent states in which the identity and power of each is a reflection of the identity and power of all states in the federation. The European Union and NATO are examples of such a federation. Its weakness is that if other federations and stand-alone states exist, warfare remains a possibility. In other words, the Us-Them dichotomy has not been obliterated.

Mead's ultimate solution is to establish a series of autonomous organizations in every corner of the globe that would have separate but complementary responsibilities for the essentials of life, such as the production of food and the protection of the environment, as well as more prosaic functions such as communications, banking, and policing. In order to mitigate against the possibility of clusters of such associations joining forces to create an asymmetric power base, each of them should foster its own unique identity, and no two organizations should be alike in properties such as size and structure. Although Mead does not mention the United Nations, the impression created is that she is calling for an end run around it. Her vision is that of a leaderless ("acephalous," in anthropological jargon) organizational arrangement reminiscent of what prevailed in hunting and gathering societies. Little wonder she was renowned for tying anthropological insights about pre-industrial society to the contemporary world.

Towards the end of her essay Mead proposes the establishment of a global secondary language, simple enough so that ideally every human being could learn to speak, read, and write it. Marvellous it would be if such a language could be institutionalized, but the fate of Esperanto is well known, and sceptics might wonder if this innovative suggestion is impractical, and whether her entire vision of a world order devoid of central power and leadership is any different. All that I can say is that I have not encountered any proposals about how to improve on the United Nations that are more imaginative than Mead's.

Koch

In *War and Peace in Jalémó* (1974) Koch focused on conflict and its resolution in an isolated New Guinea foraging society. His main conclusion was that the reason that disputes escalated into war was the absence of effective local mechanisms to resolve them, especially third party intervention, which he regarded as indispensable for creating harmony both in small-scale societies and the modern state.

According to Koch there was no central political authority in Jalémó. Social order rested on the patterns of kinship and residence. Descent was traced in the male line, and men often married women from lineages beyond the community, creating inter-village bonds. Another feature of social organization was a men's hut composed of several separate lineages. Although there were no ascribed positions of authority or even achieved ones with clout, respected elders had influence, and there were "big men" renowned for their personal attributes and accomplishments (e.g., as hunters). Common to New Guinea in the past, pigs occupied a special position in virtually all important relations among the Jalé. Pig exchange accompanied marital and ceremonial occasions and was the pivotal element in peace negotiations between warring factions.

Koch explains that the main types of conflict among the Jalé in ascending order of gravity were the English equivalents of altercation, scuffle, and warfare. An altercation was a minor argument or shouting match aired in public. A scuffle emerged when an altercation was expanded into a physical confrontation such as kicking and stone throwing. In both cases, the weight of kinship and residence helped to suppress them, and allies of the opponents, elders, and big men routinely urged restraint; in addition, songs reminiscent of Inuit culture aired and lightened grievances (70–1).

Contributing to a timely resolution was the practice of avoidance. Rivals sometimes ceased to communicate and associate with each other, and in some cases one of the parties simply relocated to a different village. The most extreme expression of avoidance was suicide. According to Koch (75), suicide was occasionally resorted to as a method of revenge against one's foes, leaving them troubled by guilt and regret.

Fieldwork among the isolated and apparently truculent Jalé, who displayed little willingness to cooperate with the anthropologist, was not a tea party, making the high quality of his ethnography all the more impressive. However, as the author himself points out (26), quarrels and disputes are a normal part of social life. Why, then, make such a fuss about the altercations and scuffles that would appear to be universal? Koch's answer presumably would reflect the concerns of Jalé people themselves: altercations can turn into scuffles and scuffles into warfare.

This brings me to a critical comment. Koch describes Jalémó warfare (76–7) as an intermittent, hit-and-miss operation (with time out for tending the gardens) that occasionally mobilized numerous warriors but more often only small scattered groups or individual forays into enemy territory. Even if the sources of enmity were serious offences such as assassination or pig theft or debt that demanded retaliation, this looks much more to me like feud rather than war, or possibly only vendetta, which is a more restricted and individual phenomenon.

Jalé society was not devoid of local mechanisms for reducing conflict. Social organization and deliberate intervention, including the third-party variety, played a role. Yet Koch labels these mechanisms feeble (32), and the reason is clear. Concerned individuals could urge belligerents to see reason, but nobody had the authority to force them to back down; in other words there was an in-built incapacity to prevent scuffles from escalating into what the author described as warfare.

The solution, according to Koch, was the introduction of third-party intervention with sufficient power and authority to impose order and harmony. His suggestion (158) that an outside (colonial?) power could readily pacify Jalémó and its neighbours is correct. Such action might eventually encourage centralized authority to take root in Jalémó. But then it no longer would be Jalémó – an egalitarian society of hunters and gatherers.

In closing, a few words about the author's claim that third-party intervention, or the shift from dyadic to triadic mechanisms of conflict resolution, is just as critical for contemporary international relations as it is in isolated foraging communities. This might appear to be a superfluous claim, because surely third-party intervention finds its most elaborate expression (and opposition to self-help or vigilante justice) in the modern state and broader entities such as the United Nations. Yet while the state ideally is a source of order and justice, it also is a coercive organization reflecting its reservoir of institutional power. Here it is instructive to recall Max Weber's famous definition of the state (1949, 154): "a compulsory political association that has a monopoly over the legitimate use of force within a given territory."

As for the United Nations, Koch dismisses it as toothless, because it lacks the authority to force compliance among its member states and because it is composed of individual states that retain their parochial interests. Only if the world community agrees to replace national interests by common interests, he argues, can an effective replacement of the UN – a supranational government (174) – emerge.

Koch applauds Margaret Mead for paving the way to humanity's New Jerusalem with her vision of autonomous specialized associations located around the globe that together provide the essentials of human existence. Yet this vision is not enough. To make it come true, both Mead and Koch agree, a radical organizational change must first be implemented: the nation state must be dismantled and deposited into the dustbin of history.

Fry

We may not be able to judge a book by its cover, and sometimes not even by its title (*The Lamb and the Tiger* inconveniently comes to mind), but *The Human Potential for Peace* (2006) by Douglas Fry captures the essence of his message. His starting point is to challenge the widespread assumption that humans are hyper-aggressive, war-loving creatures, because their genetic inheritance has made them that way. His contrary argument is that peace and cooperation rather than conflict and competition have dominated human interaction throughout history; moreover, when disputes and aggression do break out, they usually are stifled by a rich range of in-built mechanisms found in all societies, from hunters and gatherers to tribes, chiefdoms, and the modern state.

Consider the following quotations: "The human potential for peace is underappreciated whereas violence and war … are overemphasized, exaggerated and thus *naturalized*" (2); "Inevitably war becomes a self-fulfilling prophecy" (251); "Warfare is not a natural, inevitable part of human nature" (247 and 262); "The central fallacy is that *warfare* is an evolutionary adaptation" (217); "As an institution, war is already obsolete" (247); in the era of nuclear weapons, resorting to military force when confronted with security concerns "is like trying to perform heart surgery with a chainsaw" (xiii); "There is bountiful anthropological evidence that the label *peacemaking primate*, on balance, is far more fitting an appellation than is *killer-ape*" (251).

Although towards the end of his book Fry turns his attention to the challenge of fashioning peace in the current era of nuclear weapons and nation state rivalry, his primary focus is on hunters and gatherers. This is appropriate for two reasons. First, 99 per cent of human existence (20) has been spent in nomadic bands. Second, if warfare is natural rather than a cultural invention, abundant evidence of it should be apparent in this earliest form of human social organization.

I now turn to three of Fry's most significant insights. It will be recalled that Shaw and Wong in *Genetic Seeds of Warfare* promoted an image of hunters and gatherers inhabiting tightly knit communities closed off from and hostile to neighbouring bands, with rampant xenophobia the predictable consequence. Drawing his evidence from the ethnographic record of such societies all around the globe, Fry shows that this image could hardly be more misleading. Bands tend to be loosely arranged, unsegmented collections of people, marked by egalitarianism rather than centralized authority, the membership of which expands and shrinks regularly as individuals periodically relocate to other villages. Smoothing their way are a number of cross-cutting ties based on marriage, friendship, and at times trade. This image of bands as quasi-amorphous groups in constant flux, and the ties among them that enhance amicable interaction, fly in the face of the portrait of the highly integrated, stable community that eyeballs its neighbours as enemies. Summing up, Fry observes (168), "Shaw and Wong's 'nucleus ethnic group' simply doesn't exist."

A second insight concerns the precise nature of hostile interaction between bands. Fry does not deny that strained relations often emerge within a band, or that the same occurs between bands. What he strenuously objects to is the tendency in the literature to label inter-band combat a form of war. The reality, he explains (170), is that combat usually is between individuals, not groups (217), and certainly not kin groups. This is because in band social organization relationships among kin tend to be weak and loose (iii).

Fry expresses similar dissatisfaction with the label "feud" when it is stuck on band societies. Feud is a kin-based form of hostility, and only when social organization is segmented into tribes with kinship lineages does feud make its appearance. When that happens, so does something else: whereas in hostilities between bands, revenge and counter-revenge are usually between specific individuals, in tribal feuds the target is expanded to include the enemy's kin.

Fry also takes exception to the tendency in the past among scholars to describe hostilities between Australian Aborigines as warfare. More recent literature, as Fry points out (148–58), demonstrates that war was rare, and what passed for it could more precisely be defined as feud, or in some cases just individual self-redress. For Aborigines, war aimed at territorial and cultural conquest made little sense. Land was plentiful, population density low, and as nomads what would the victors do with captured opponents or additional perishable food supplies? Besides, like hunters and gatherers elsewhere, Aboriginal bands intermingled frequently, the result more often than not being friendship rather than belligerence.

I now turn to Fry's third important insight. In a nutshell, the entire notion that hunters and gatherers lack mechanisms to reduce conflict is, in his view, erroneous. Surely the cross-cutting ties that link bands together qualify as such a mechanism, but Fry has something much more specific in mind. Referring to the work of several anthropologists, including Koch's (23), he lists five widespread approaches to the management of conflict: avoidance, toleration, negotiation, third-party intervention, and self-redress or self-help. The first three are consistent with the practices of foragers, but what about the triadic option? Here Fry parts company with Koch. His argument is that third-party intervention occurs in *all* societies, including foragers; it is the rule rather than the exception (7, 22). In his words (107), "The third party roles of friendly peacemaker and mediator are widespread in the ethnographic spectrum." In Koch's defence, these mechanisms lack the capacity to demand compliance that is institutionalized into centralized authority roles.

Self-help appears to be an outrider in this list. It is resorted to when an individual confronts an aggressor. In other words, it seals the hostility between rivals. Fry points out that self-redress is most prevalent among hunters and gatherers and diminishes steadily as social organization evolves through tribes, chiefdoms, and the state. In tribes kinship is the unit of combat, in chiefdoms there are standing armies and leaders to direct them, while in the state self-help would be labelled illegitimate vigilante justice.

Fry's survey of the ethnographic record revealed eighty societies, representing the main stages of social organization, which have been overwhelmingly peaceful (81); Iceland, he points out (96), has been at peace for 700 years. Fry also (95) identified seventy non-warring societies. Why the latter number is not the same as that of the peaceful societies is curious. So too in this context is his rather perplexing remark (96): "Most known cultures do engage in warfare, but some do not." While I'm in a critical mood, perhaps it should be pointed out that Fry has selected only ethnographic examples that support his basic thesis, perhaps a forgivable flaw because he was bucking the mainstream intellectual current.

Fry wraps up his study by turning his attention to the threats facing peace in the contemporary world and how to defuse them. He points out that international relations today are similar to band societies in that self-help predominates in rivalries between nation states. Each nation acts in its own interests, even if that means going to war, confident that there is no superior authority to constrain it.

His solutions to this tragic scene (248) include fostering crosscutting relations between nations, acknowledging global interdependence, establishing new values and attitudes that promote peace, and expanding and empowering global governance. A couple of these might strike us as platitudes, but increasing ties among nations makes sense. Especially important, Fry suggests, is for societal leaders to spend time in hostile nations and encourage their children to do the same; the resulting reduction of ethnocentrism on all sides and the presence of "peace hostages" (253) in enemy territory might undermine the attraction of war.

Most significant of all is Fry's emphasis on expanding and strengthening global governance. Unlike Mead and Koch, who urged the demise of the nation state and sidestepping the UN by re-organizing the institutions that fulfil basic human needs, Fry's recommendations are decidedly modest: make better use of third-party conflict management such as mediation, arbitration, and adjudication; render the United Nations more effective by increasing the authority of the secretary-general (259), and rethink the collective benefit of the veto enjoyed by the superpowers. A further recommendation is to replace the International Court of Justice's limited power of arbitration with a mandate not only to judge who is guilty, but also to enforce its decisions with appropriate penalties; in other words, to shift its focus to adjudication.

Whether or not these recommendations are plausible is debatable, mainly because rationality and sheer common sense seem to be in such short supply. If they weren't, the globe's nations would be frantic over the crippling conflicts and wars that pop up regularly, despite the backdrop of potential nuclear annihilation; and they would rally en masse around a strengthened United Nations and World Court rather than complain about minor deficiencies and clumsy bureaucracies.

It is as if humanity had been confined to a time capsule, unable to remember the past or imagine the future, conscious only of the troubled present, which was regarded as natural and immutable. In this context, Canada's renewed commitment to peacekeeping is not likely to have much impact. It may well be overwhelmed by the dubious mindset that accepts war as the indelible mark of the species.

I can almost sense the reader's relief (and my own) as I return now to Fry's rosier perspective. *The Human Potential for Peace*, constructed around the author's impressive command of the ethnographic record, is a book whose time has come, if only to make people realize that aggression is not all that can be read into humanity's past and future. Not surprisingly, Fry ends on a hopeful note:

humans have an enormous capacity for peace, restraint and harmony are preferred over extreme aggression, most conflicts are resolved without bloodshed, and if slavery could be abolished, so too can war (217, 247, 259). His final words (263): "Abolishing war in the 21st century is not only realistic in the sense that it is possible, but also realistically necessary for human survival and well-being. The peacemaking primate has the capacity to do so."

Mechanisms in Pre-industrial Societies to Reduce Strain

Inuit Singing Duels

Individuals fight each other with words rather than physically, the more insulting and scornful the better (Hoebel 1954). Although there were variations on the procedure from group to group, generally the person whose songs are deemed by the audience the more clever and devastating, and who maintains his temper, is the winner.

Lethal and Non-Lethal Weapons

In some cultures such as the Nuer in Africa the choice of weapons depended on whether the conflict was external or internal. When engaged in battle with outsiders, weapons that kill were used, but fights between Nuer individuals dictated non-lethal weapons. Obviously this was a limited mechanism, because while it benefited the Nuer it probably exacerbated hostility with its neighbours.

Witchcraft

It sublimates strain away from everyday interaction into the non-empirical realm. In cultures like the Azande where the supernatural and natural worlds are fused, when misfortune strikes such as a hunting accident or child's death, blame often shifts from individual human beings to the evil machinations of witches. Of course, this is not a perfect solution, because the focus then turns to a search for the identity of the witches, who more often than not are assumed to be close associates or relatives of the victims. Sorcery, incidentally, is even less effective as a safety valve, because it involves the intentional usage of charms and poisons by flesh-and-blood specialists who can be hired to affect a person's fortunes, usually negatively.[2]

Exchange of Umbilical Cords

Among some Aborigines in Australia as well as the inhabitants of the Andaman Islands near Thailand, potential enemies from feuding clans exchanged the umbilical cords of their newborn children. As these individuals grew up, they became institutionalized best friends and trading partners, thus creating social links between otherwise hostile groups.

Joking Relations

Built-in-strain between in-laws appears to be a universal human condition. The Andamanese had three ways to cope with it. One was avoidance; in-laws simply kept out of each other's way. Another was extreme mutual respect, restraint, and formality when the parties did come into contact with each other. The third was exactly the opposite: ritualized disrespect or joking relations. In this version, in-laws cursed, mocked, and insulted each other, but because such behaviour was culturally prescribed, and because the verbal exchanges followed a formula, the quality of in-law interaction was not diminished.[3]

Cross-Cutting Ties

A variation on the theme of cross-cutting ties as a source of amicable relationships that reduce strain has been proposed by Max Gluckman (1956). His argument, which has universal implications, is that conflict itself is the basis of societal integration. He points out that an individual has multiple contacts with different people that sometimes clash. However, strain in one sphere tends to be cancelled by harmony in another. For example, two people may disagree violently about politics yet share the same religion. Gluckman's conclusion is that not only is conflict normal, but as a social relationship it is a source of communication that ultimately is positive, because it is balanced and rendered neutral by one's numerous and complex associations, with societal cohesion the happy outcome.

Kula Ring

One of the most famous cultural innovations that addressed conflict was the *kula* ring in the Trobriand Islands east of New Guinea, cleverly analysed by Malinowski ([1922] 1961). It consisted of the ceremonial exchange of necklaces and armbands from one island to the next. These items had little intrinsic value, but their exchange increased interaction between residents of the different islands who were inclined to be mutually hostile. This in turn paved the way for bartering activity that did involve valuable goods such as fish and pottery. It is significant that individuals who exchanged necklaces and armbands were not permitted to engage in bartering, but they were free to do so with others. In this way the ceremonial and economic dimensions of the kula ring were not confused and possibly compromised.

Fictive Kinship

In many societies kinship connections extend far beyond biology and marriage. Here we find classificatory kinship in which literally hundreds of individuals are recognized as one's brothers, sisters, or parents. Especially important is widespread grandparent and grandchild terminology, because the interaction between alternative generations is usually harmonious. In feuding societies such as Corsica, the prevalence of godparenthood helped to suppress strain, and it is noteworthy that peace pacts were usually concluded with a forced marriage between members of the feuding families.

Incest Taboo and Circulation of Women

Probably the most significant and universal mechanism that generates solidarity in society begins with the incest taboo and ends up creating a category of relationships based on marriage (affines), as distinct from blood relationships (consanguines). Referred to variably as alliance or exchange theory, a truly innovative and powerful perspective established by one of the most brilliant anthropologists, Lévi-Strauss ([1949] 1969), the incest taboo is portrayed as the mechanism that catapulted *Homo sapiens* from a state of nature to culture.

Because marriage to various degrees of people related by blood was proscribed, it was necessary to find marriage partners beyond the family unit. To employ the language of the perspective, women were pumped out of one community to become marital partners in another community, and the latter eventually pumped back women into the original community.

Alliance theory is more complicated than the foregoing description, especially because rather than a reciprocal and direct exchange of women between two communities, usually a succession of exchanges involving several communities transpires before the original wife-giving community is compensated with its own supply of eligible marital partners. The overall result is to generate solidarity among groups and reinforce the integrity of society.

Philosopher

In an earlier chapter, reference was made to Canadian philosopher John McMurtry's analysis of the overlap between war and football. I now turn to his highly innovative monograph, *Understanding War* (1988). McMurtry lays out a two-step procedure for putting an end to war as we know it and ushering in a new era of global cooperation. A key distinction in the monograph is between pathological and non-pathological war. The former is war in its conventional sense from the time of Sun Tzu to the present, and I shall start with it.

McMurtry argues that it makes no sense to condemn the soldier on the battlefield – even the Nazi – because he (or she) is blameless, a mere puppet acting out a role generated by the encapsulating social structure. The social structure is the instrument of the ruling group, which increasingly takes the form of a marriage between big business and the military. McMurtry pays special attention to the lucrative arms industry (35) and concludes that the arms race continues to expand because it serves ruling-class interests (37), namely power and wealth. Near the end of the monograph the author raises an alarm about the degree to which civilian populations have become controlled by state-directed militaries, which he describes (44–5) as the "hidden, crystallizing pattern of our global social order." Pointing out that the greatest threat to citizens is often their own military acting under the direction of self-interested ruling groups, McMurtry wraps up his analysis with the charge that the real enemy of humankind is nothing less than the military system itself. The destruction of that system is the first step towards the victory of peace over war.

Intrinsic to the second step is the distinction between pathological and non-pathological wars. From McMurtry's perspective there are no *natural* human enemies; contests between humans are cultural and political products reflecting ruling-group power and interests. There are, however, natural *non-human* enemies such as pestilence, plagues, diseases like cancer, and environmental degradation. War pitting humans against each other is pathological, because it kills human beings. McMurtry's imaginative solution is not to get rid of war per se, but instead to redirect it towards natural non-human enemies. This form of war is non-pathological, because it saves rather than destroys human lives. It will be recalled that in Shaw and Wong's genetic approach to war, the Us-Them dichotomy was portrayed as beneficial at each stage of human organization until the advent of nuclear weapons. In sharp contrast, McMurtry (44) describes the dichotomy as possibly the most dangerous prejudice that has ever existed. If humankind rallies en masse around the war on natural non-human enemies, that prejudice will have finally run its course.

On an abstract level, McMurtry's analysis is powerful and innovative, but on a practical level he has little to say about how the military system could be demolished, or how the world community could be persuaded to abandon pathological war and unite in the battle against natural threats to its survival.

My own solutions are much more modest (maybe overly so). Although after the Second World War Costa Rica (Fry 2006, 96) scrapped its military, it is improbable that Canada or any other nation will finally follow suit any time soon. That being the case, let us rehabilitate the sane policy of mobilizing our troops only for defence as a last resort when diplomacy fails, and let us do what we can to revive international interest in the reduction of weapons of mass destruction and in peaceful coexistence.

It also is improbable that capitalism is going to be abandoned. That being the case, let us recognize, along with Boutros Boutros-Ghali, that inequality is the principal source of social problems in the world. The solution is to eradicate the enormous gap in nations such as the United States and increasingly in Canada between the haves and have-nots. Of course, defenders of that gap argue that it is necessary in order to motivate the giants of industry, whose wealth trickles down in the form of employment and disposable income to the lower ranks. My answer is that, except for a few driven and greedy individuals, it is not the amount of remuneration on which motivation depends; otherwise how to explain the much more modest gap between CEO and worker in previous eras? Equally effective are clear signals that differentiate the boss and the labourer in the hierarchy of an organization. Some degree of unequal remuneration is one of them, probably the most significant in a capitalist setting, but it is not the only signal. Rewards can also be non-monetary. Honorific titles and awards and the size of one's office or the view out the window can convey a sense of power and accomplishment just as readily as the size of one's bonus. As for trickle-down economics, the desperation of the middle class in advanced industrial societies undermines that self-serving elite assumption.

These comments are aimed mostly at the renowned 1 per cent. I am perfectly aware that in the middle ranks of corporations, individuals often work extremely hard under stressful conditions and arguably deserve their above-average incomes. Perhaps the day will finally arrive when the model society is defined as one that imposes a ceiling on the annual incomes of CEOs in conjunction with more robust policies of income redistribution. Surprising it would be if the general opinion is that my solutions are even more dreamy than those of our esteemed philosopher.

Poet

If philosophical reflection, regardless of its profundity and genius for identifying the real enemy of war as well as its solution, is too abstract (at least in the short run) to serve as a practical guide, there always is *Lysistrata* (Aristophanes 2003), a comic play first performed in Athens in 411 BCE. The heroine, after whom the play is named, fed up with the interminable Peloponnesian War, latches on to a novel remedy. She persuades women across the country to withhold sexual privileges from their husbands and lovers until they agree to peace negotiations. The play unfolds with the frustrations of men clearly evident by their erections and concludes with their eventual capitulation to the demands of Lysistrata and her followers. Whether philosophers, presumably aroused more by logic than amour, would place any value on Lysistrata's strategy is beyond my knowledge.

Such has been the impact of *Lysistrata* that numerous adaptations – not only for plays but also for opera, ballet, and musicals – appeared throughout the twentieth century and continue to entertain audiences in the twenty-first century. The difference is that the new versions often attribute to Lysistrata a greater feminist and anti-war consciousness than apparently was intended by Aristophanes. It might be added that the spectre of peace-loving, anti-war women clashes with the contemporary reality of women in the armed forces.

I opened this book with a quotation from William Blake's "Tiger" and shall close it with one of his other memorable poems.

Mock on, mock on, Voltaire, Rousseau;
Mock on, mock on, 'tis all in vain!
You throw the sand against the wind,
And the wind blows it back again.

This poem reflects Blake's impatience with the Enlightenment values of rationalism, universalism, empiricism, secularism, liberalism, and growing scientific domination.[4] To a considerable extent the clash between the Enlightenment and the counter-Enlightenment values of community, faith, subjectivity, nationalism, conservatism, and tradition has been the story of this study, indeed one of the background tensions between war and peace.

Over the stretch of recent history the values of the Enlightenment and the counter-Enlightenment have usually coexisted and overlapped. Had it been otherwise, human beings, that most complex of creatures, would have ceased to be fully human. Periodically, however, these opposed visions are polarized, and the result is caricature. For example, globalization, the offspring of Enlightenment rationality and progress, supposedly was the engine that would lift all of humanity into unprecedented wealth. Yet it has benefited multinational corporations and economic elites much more than the masses of ordinary citizens. It also was one of the sources of new expressions of heterogeneity such as the small nationalisms that inflamed pockets of the globe in places like the Balkans.

The counter-Enlightenment, in turn, with its emotional attachment to community and kin, arguably prepared the soil for Nazism and Fascism and fostered the in-group/out-group hostility that Shaw-Wong and Huntington identified (but failed to condemn) as the principal cause of aggression and war over the ages. The most bizarre recent examples of the counter-Enlightenment, it might be suggested, are Brexit in Britain and America under the spell of Donald Trump.

For many thoughtful people our apparent incapacity to resolve the differences between opposed paradigms once and for all, and surmount the eternal Us-Them dichotomy, may well constitute one of the deep philosophical mysteries of the species. For others, there is no mystery, if only because dualism or binary opposition appears to be an intrinsic propensity of the human brain (Needham 1973). Be that as it may, the challenge of our times is decidedly more mundane and immediate because now the threat of catastrophic global warming has been added to potential nuclear annihilation. Thus the critical question: how to persuade humanity that in the face of this double whammy the spectre of war is more unimaginable and pernicious than ever before?

My guess is that resistance to this overture will be especially pronounced among societal elites, a portion of which has no doubt profited from war. Societal elites (at least some of them) may believe – if in fact they accept the evidence of species vulnerability – that their wealth and power will enable them to endure both nuclear war and potentially irreversible global warming, perhaps by retreating behind barricades of technologically sophisticated restricted zones. Such are the origins of human fantasies. The vast bulk of the rest of humanity, especially the impoverished, will be more amenable to a world without war. This is not because they are by nature less aggressive, envious, or avaricious than those higher on the totem pole. Rather it is because they will lack the resources to cope with calamity and because they usually have been fodder or puppets in wars, not the influential civilians and generals who have launched and led them. For people who struggle to survive from one day to the next, war only adds to their misery. What they dream about and crave is adequate food and shelter, a life-sustaining environment, and the melody of contented children at play rather than the rumble of armies on the move.

Notes

2. Peaceful Kingdom

1 Dorn (2005) indicates 1947 as the date of Canada's first UN mission (in Korea).
2 See also Winslow (1999). Much of this article already appeared in her book, especially chapter 4.
3 Dorn (2005) credits a Canadian soldier, Brigadier-General Lewis Mackenzie, for easing tensions early in the Bosnia campaign by his skilful use of the media. Mackenzie tells his own story in *Peacekeeper: The Road to Sarajevo* (1993).
4 Actually, during the Cold War none of the permanent members of the Security Council were allowed to participate in UN peacekeeping operations. The assumption was that their national interests rendered them too biased for the job. By the 1990s, all this had changed. The permanent members had taken the lead in dealing with hotspots around the globe, in the process converting peacekeeping into a largely military exercise.
5 Until I read Pearson's book, I had regarded him as a decent and engaging human being somewhat lacking in profundity. The depth of his insights about world politics has led me to a much greater appreciation of the man.

3. Warrior Nation

1 As a measure of the respect that Hillier enjoyed at Fort Hood, he and his wife were appointed honorary citizens of Texas.

2 According to Staples (2006, 21), Martin eventually realized he had been duped.

3 For a tour de force of the Harper government's assaults on civil society, see Barlow (2015).

4 Gender will be considered in much greater detail in chapter 6.

5 Having felt deeply about some of the moral issues in my past research projects, especially poverty, racism, and anti-Semitism, I sympathize with the strong feelings expressed by Granatstein and Bercuson in their support of the military and right-wing politics. The challenge is how to establish a dialogue, when to compromise means to sacrifice one's principles.

6 Reflect on Nadeau's cheeky comment (2011, 101): "Poverty is a symptom of government dysfunction."

7 After Hillier retired, he was courted by the Liberals as a candidate for their party. In view of his negative attitudes towards both Parliament and the civil service, it is not surprising that he declined.

8 He was not always optimistic. During the decade of darkness he considered resigning from the armed forces.

9 Justin Trudeau is an example of the routinization of charisma.

10 Both Nadeau (2011) and Clark (2013) have argued that Harper is not a true friend of Israel because such a friend would not hesitate to criticize his ally when bad behaviour warrants it. This strikes me as possibly correct in an abstract sense, but rather meaningless in terms of the loyalty expected between friends.

11 Jeffrey (2015, 46) has reported that as far back as Harper's student days at the University of Calgary, he attended a summer training camp in the United States for young Republicans.

4. Genetic Basis of War

1 The technical term is epigenesis.

2 This, of course, is my overview of their study. In the interests of clarity I have slid over some of the nuances such as the genetic component of proximate causes and the closer connection of xenophobia to the genetic base of the model in comparison with ethnocentrism.

3 Incidentally, by suggesting that culture may have been transformed into the critical societal force, I do not wish to imply that there is anything new about culture per se. At every stage of social organization, from the state back through tribes, bands, and indeed the small nucleus ethnic group, culture thrived.

5. Cultural Basis of War

1   It is curious that in Canada and the United States in the 1980s a religious movement took hold among far-right groups such as the Ku Klux Klan called "Identity," which asked the very question that Huntington considers most fundamental to humans: who are we? Identity's answer is that the racists and anti-Semites are white Christians, the creators and guardians of civilization. Just as post–Cold War cultural identity supposedly provides people with a sense of confidence and direction, the movement called Identity did the same for members of the extreme right (see Barrett 1987, 335–6).

2   Huntington is undecided whether an eighth civilization, Africa, should be included in the list. It should be added that as Huntington points out (44), several prominent scholars have produced their own lists of civilizations.

3   Huntington refers briefly (31) to Francis Fukuyama's well-known study (1992) in which it is argued that with the Soviet Union's collapse and the triumph of Western liberalism, the entire globe has ground to a stop; in other words, history has run its course. *The Clash* amounts to a forceful repudiation of Fukuyama, who actually had been one of Huntington's former students – an intriguing reversal of the usual assumption in academia that it is the young who devour their elders.

4   In 1990 Bernard Lewis, a reputed expert on Islam, published "The Roots of Muslim Rage," in which he used the expression "the clash of civilizations," possibly the source for Huntington's title. In his later book, *What Went Wrong?* (2002) Lewis celebrates the past achievements and glory of Islamic society, but his explanation of what went wrong and how it can be fixed is not very satisfactory: Islam's decline due to its inadequate reception to Western culture, and the solution based on relinquishing the search for scapegoats and embracing Western democracy.

5   There is a catchy expression that patriotism is the last refuge of the scoundrel. Perhaps, then, Canadians should count their blessings for not being like America in this respect. Yet there is little doubt that Canadian patriotism is a largely unarticulated but nevertheless real force below the surface. I vividly recall the surprise among some of my American academic friends at the expressions of patriotism among Canadians at the time of the Free Trade negotiations with the United States. To my knowledge not a single newspaper produced the obvious headline: Canadian Home-Grown Scoundrels Exposed!

6 Ashraf (2012, 525) suggests that the clash of civilizations thesis and the danger it implied was a godsend for lobbyists in the U.S. armaments industry.

7 Huntington died in 2008.

8 To be candid, there has been a similar power gap between the anthropologist and research subject in the majority of research projects.

9 For example, in 1950 (see González 2004, 11) the AAA leadership secretly provided the CIA with a list of its members and information about their research interests.

10 Britain also established a version of HTS for deployment in Afghanistan called the Defence Cultural Specialist Unit.

11 It was the Vietnam War that prompted the AAA in 1971 to release its first formal statement on ethics.

12 Not all members of the AAA were liberals or left wing. In 1991 conservative members (Price 2004, 67) proposed that the organization issue a formal public statement in support of the Iraq War.

13 Price's important book is dedicated to Laura Nader, who, more than anyone else, encouraged anthropologists to study up. Her work influenced my decision in a study of the radical right in Canada to focus on the racists rather than their victims and confronted me with the same uncomfortable questions about ethics.

14 A sharp distinction should be made between the silliness of campus feuds and the sometimes acrimonious but important debates about issues such as corporate and military funding.

6. Gender, Aboriginals, and Resistance

1 One of my aunts served as a nurse in the navy. Life was a struggle for this fine woman after the war. She eventually died of a drug overdose, but whether PTSD was involved is beyond my knowledge.

2 The Commonwealth Institute operated from 1962 until 2002. In 2007 the Commonwealth Educational Trust assumed some of its previous functions.

3 The one-time right to vote in a federal election was granted to First Nation soldiers in 1917.

4 In 2010 the government, after showing it could not be pushed around by the UN, signed the declaration.

5 A much more detailed and nuanced account of the Oka Crisis is found in Zig Zag (a pseudonym) (2007). See also Marshall (2014).

6 For more details about the Ipperwash Crisis, see Marshall (2016).

7 Peter Carstens (1971), my mentor in anthropology at the University of Toronto, pointed out that the reserve system in Canada was similar to the Bantustans or homelands during the apartheid era in his natal country, South Africa.

8 Also worthy of mention is the earlier Berger Report (1977), which investigated the proposed Mackenzie Valley pipeline in British Columbia. It recommended a ten-year moratorium on resource extraction and development projects in order to determine the potential impact on the environment and First Nation communities.

7. Lamb Power and Tiger Power

1 Granatstein (2007, 60) does acknowledge that capitalism must be subjected to some degree of control. He also recognizes that the Canadian state is rendered more viable by the provision of universal health care and even equalization payments to the less wealthy provinces. The implication is that he may not entirely fit the new warrior label attached to him by McKay and Swift.

2 The main ethnographic source for the Nuer and the Azande is Evans-Pritchard (1937 and 1940), one of the early giants in the discipline.

3 The main ethnographic source for the Andaman Islands is Radcliffe-Brown (1922), another early giant in anthropology.

4 It is curious that Blake includes Rousseau in this poem, because arguably he fits just as well in the counter-Enlightenment camp (see Melzer 1996).

Bibliography

Amato, Peter. 2002. "Hobbes, Darwinism, and Conceptions of Human Nature." *Minerva: An Internet Journal of Philosophy* 6:24–50.

American Anthropological Association. 2007. "Statement on HTS," 31 October.

Anderson, Doris. 2006. "Status of Women." *Canadian Encyclopedia.*

Anker, Lane. 2005. "Peacekeeping and Public Opinion." *Canadian Military Journal* 6 (2): 23–32.

Aristophanes. 2003. Translated by Sarah Ruden. Indianapolis, IN: Hackett Publishing.

Ashraf, Mian Muhammad Tahir. 2012. "The Clash of Civilizations? A Critique." *Pakistan Journal of Social Sciences* 32 (2): 512–27.

Barlow, Maude. 2015. *Broken Covenant.* Ottawa: Council of Canadians.

Barrett, Stanley R. 1987. *Is God a Racist? The Right Wing in Canada.* Toronto: University of Toronto Press.

– 1994. *Paradise.* Toronto: University of Toronto Press.

– 1996. *Anthropology: A Student's Guide to Theory and Methods.* Toronto: University of Toronto Press.

– 2002. *Culture Meets Power.* Westport, CT: Praeger.

Barth, Fredrik. 1959. *Political Leadership among Swat Pathans.* London: Athlone.

Beeby, Dean. 2015. "Secret Status of Women Report Paints Grim Picture for Canada." CBC News, 7 September.

Bell, Martin. 1996. *In Harm's Way: Reflections of a War-Zone Thug.* London: Penguin.

Bercuson, David. 1996. *Significant Incident: Canada's Army, the Airborne, and the Murder in Somalia.* Toronto: McClelland and Stewart.

Bercuson, David, and J.L. Granatstein. 2011. *Lessons Learned?* Calgary: Canadian Defence and Foreign Affairs Institute.

Berger, T.R. 1977. *Northern Frontier, Northern Homeland: Report of the Mackenzie Valley Pipeline Inquiry.* Ottawa: Supply and Services Canada.

Berndt, R.M. 1962. *Excess and Restraint: Social Control among a New Guinea Mountain People*. Chicago: University of Chicago Press.

Bourrie, Mark. 2015. *Kill the Messengers: Stephen Harper's Assault on Your Right to Know*. Toronto: HarperCollins Publishers.

Boutros-Ghali, Boutros. 1992. "An Agenda for Peace." Report of the Secretary-General, 17 June. https://doi.org/10.1177/004711789201100302.

Bray, Richard. 2011. "The Battlespace of Culture: Mapping the Human Terrain." *Vanguard*, 1 January.

Broad, William J., and David E. Sanger. 2016. "U.S. Shifts Focus to Smaller Nuclear Bombs." *International New York Times*, 13 January.

Bronskill, Jim, and Michael Tutton. 2015. "Harper: 'Way Past the Time' for Missing, Murdered, Aboriginal Women Inquiry." Canadian Press, 6 October.

Brooks, David. 2011. "Huntington's Clash Revisited." *New York Times*, 3 March.

Bryden, Joan. 2016. "PM Says Ottawa Faces Hard Choices." *Toronto Star*, 23 August.

Buechert, Michael. 2011. "Canada as Peacemaker: Myth or Reality?" *Project Peacemakers*, 6 October.

Campion-Smith, Bruce, and Les Whittington. 2008. "Headline," *Toronto Star* 16 April.

Canada. 1969. *Statement of the Government of Canada on Indian Policy*. Ottawa: Queen's Printer.

Canadian Press. 2016. "Chiefs Say Proposed Algonquin Land Claim Deal Illegal, Fraudulent," 4 March.

Cardinal, Harold. 1969. *The Unjust Society*. Vancouver: Douglas & McIntyre.

CBC News Online. 2006. "Aboriginals and the Canadian Military," 21 June.

– 2013. "Nine Questions about Idle No More," 5 June.

Chenier, Nancy Miller. 2006. "Women and War." *Canadian Encyclopedia*.

Clark, Joe. 2013. *How We Lead: Canada in a Century of Change*. Toronto: Random House Canada.

von Clausewitz, Carl. (1832) 2007. *On War*. Oxford: Oxford University Press.

Counts, Dorothy. 1991. "Suicide in Different Ages from a Cross-cultural Perspective." In *Life Perspectives of Suicide*, edited by Antoon Leenaars, 215–28. New York: Plenum. https://doi.org/10.1007/978-1-4899-0724 -0_15.

Crane, Stephen. 1895. *The Red Badge of Courage*. New York: D. Appleton.

Cutland, Doug. 2015. "Conservatives Treat First Nations as Disposable." *Starphoenix*, 24 July.

Dallaire, Roméo. 2004. *Shake Hands with the Devil: The Failure of Humanity in Rwanda*. Toronto: Vintage Canada.

Dash, Mike. 2011. "Dahomey's Women Warriors." Smithsonian.com, 23 September.

Dershowitz, Alan. 2003. *The Case for Israel*. Hoboken, NJ: John Wiley and Sons.

Diefenbaker, John G. 1972. *These Things We Treasure*. Toronto: Macmillan of Canada.

Dobbin, Murray. 2010. "Harper's Attack on Women's Rights and Equality." Tyee, 8 February, https://thetyee.ca/Opinion/2010/02/08/HarperWomensRights/.

Dorn, A. Walter. 2005. "Canadian Peacekeeping: Proud Tradition, Strong Future?" *Canadian Foreign Policy* 12 (2): 7–32. https://doi.org/10.1080/11926422.2005.9673396.

Dummitt, Christopher. 2012. "Lester Pearson on Trial." *Literary Review of Canada*, June, https://reviewcanada.ca/magazine/2012/06/lester-pearson-on-trial/.

Dundas, Barbara, and Serge Durflinger. n.d. "The Canadian Women's Army Corps, 1941–1946." *Dispatches*. https://www.warmuseum.ca/learn/dispatches/the-canadian-womens-army-corps-1941-1946/#tabs.

Emmet, Dorothy. 1971. "The Concept of Power." In *Power*, edited by John R. Champlin, 78–103. New York: Atherton.

Engler, Yves. 2012. *The Truth May Hurt: Lester Pearson's Peacemaking*. Blackpoint, NS: Fernwood Publishing.

Evans-Pritchard, E.E. 1937. *Witchcraft, Oracles and Magic among the Azande*. Oxford: Clarendon.

– 1940. *The Nuer*. Oxford: Clarendon.

Fanon, F. (1961) 1963. *The Wretched of the Earth*. New York: Grove.

Fenton, Cameron. 2010. "The Ethnography of an Air Strike." *Dominion* 69. http://www.dominionpaper.ca/articles/3295.

Flynn-Piercey, H. 2011. "Huntington's Clash of Civilizations." *E-International Politics*, 3 August.

Fogerty, Philippa. 2008. "Recognition at Last for Japan's Ainu." BBC News, 6 June.

Forte, Maximilian. 2008. "Canada's Own Human Terrain System: White Situational Awareness Team in Afghanistan." *Zero Anthropology*, 24 November.

Fortes, M., and E.E. Evans-Pritchard, eds. 1940. *African Political Systems*. London: Oxford University Press.

Frank, A.G. 1970. "The Development of Underdevelopment." In *Imperialism and Underdevelopment*, edited by R.I. Rhodes. New York: Monthly Review.

Fry, Douglas. 2006. *The Human Potential for Peace*. New York: Oxford University Press.

Fukuyama, Francis. 1992. *The End of History and the Last Man*. New York: Free Press.

Galbraith, John. 1983. *The Anatomy of Power*. Boston: Houghton Mifflin.

Galloway, Gloria. 2015. "Chiefs Urge Aboriginal People to Vote against Harper." *Globe and Mail*, 7 July.

Gilligan, James. 1996. *Violence*. New York: G.P. Putman's Sons.

– 2004. "Shame: The Emotions and Morality of Violence." In *Violence and Gender*, edited by P.O. Gilbert and K.K. Eby, 40–7. Upper Saddle River, NJ: Pearson Education.

Giroux, H. 2007. *The University in Chains: Confronting the Military-Industrial-Academic Complex*. Boulder, CO: Paradigm.

Gluckman, Max. 1956. *Custom and Conflict in Africa*. Oxford: Basil Blackwell.

Goldstein, Joshua. 2001. *War and Gender*. Cambridge: Cambridge University Press.

González, Roberto J., ed. 2004. *Anthropologists in the Public Sphere: Speaking Out on War, Peace and American Power*. Austin: University of Texas Press.

– 2009. *American Counterinsurgency: Human Science and the Human Terrain*. Chicago: Prickly Paradigm.

– 2015. *The Rise and Fall of the Human Terrain System*. Oakland, CA: CounterPunch.

Granatstein, J.L. 2007. *Whose War Is It?* Toronto: HarperCollins Publishers.

Griggs, Richard. 1992. "The Meaning of 'Nation' and 'State' in the Fourth World." Occasional Paper 18. Cape Town: Center for World Indigenous Studies, University of Cape Town.

Hamandi, Ali. 2015. "For Women, Harper's Government Has Been a Disaster." iPolitics, 22 September, https://ipolitics.ca/2015/09/22/for-women-harpers-government-has-been-a-disaster/.

Harari, Oren. 2002. *The Leadership Secrets of Colin Powell*. New York: McGraw-Hill.

Hargreaves, John. 1982. "Sport and Hegemony." In *Sport, Culture and the Modern State*, edited by Hart Canleton and Richard Gruneau, 103–40. Toronto: University of Toronto Press.

Harper, Stephen. 2003. "Rediscovering the Right Agenda." *Report Magazine* 10:72–7.

– 2013. *A Great Game*. Toronto: Simon and Schuster.

Harris, M. 2014. *Party of One*. Toronto: Viking Canada.

Hawthorn, H.B., ed. 1966–7. *A Survey of the Contemporary Indians of Canada*. Ottawa: Queen's Printer.

Hedican, Edward J. 2013. *Ipperwash: The Tragic Failure of Canada's Aboriginal Policy*. Toronto: University of Toronto Press.

Hicks, Jack. 2004. "On the Application of Theories of 'Internal Colonialism' to Inuit Societies." Presentation for the Annual Conference of the Canadian Political Science Association, Winnipeg, 5 June.

Hillier, Rick. 2009. *A Soldier First*. Toronto: HarperCollins Publishers.

Hobsbawm, Eric. 1983. "Introduction: Inventing Traditions." In *The Invention of Tradition*, edited by Eric Hobsbawm and Terence Ranger, 1–14. Cambridge: Cambridge University Press.

Hoebel, E.A. 1954. *The Law of Primitive Man*. Cambridge, MA: Harvard University Press.

Horowitz, I. 1967. *The Rise and Fall of Project Camelot*. Cambridge, MA: MIT Press.

Huntington, Samuel P. 1993a. "The Clash of Civilizations?" *Foreign Affairs* 72 (3): 22–49. https://doi.org/10.2307/20045621.

– 1993b. "If Not Civilizations, What? Samuel Huntington Responds to His Critics." *Foreign Affairs* 72 (5): 191–7.

– (1996) 2003. *The Clash of Civilizations and the Remaking of World Order*. New York: Simon and Schuster.

Indian Chiefs of Alberta. 2011. "Citizens Plus." Edmonton: Indian Association of Alberta. http://ejournals.library.ualberta.ca/index.php/aps/article/view/11690/8926.

Indigenous and Northern Affairs Canada. 2014. "Aboriginal Contributions during the First World War," 24 October.

Jaschik, Scott. 2015. "U.S. Army Shuts Down Controversial Human Terrain System, Criticized by Many Anthropologists." Inside Higher Ed, 7 July. https://www.insidehighered.com/news/2015/07/07/army-shuts-down-controversial-human-terrain-system-criticized-many-anthropologists.

Jeffrey, Brooke. 2015. *Dismantling Canada*. Montreal and Kingston: McGill-Queen's University Press.

Johannsen, A. 1992. "Applied Anthropology and Post-Modern Ethnography." *Human Organization* 51 (1): 71–81. https://doi.org/10.17730/humo.51.1.t62123516285r644.

Jones, Sian. 2002. "We Won't Fight Your … Wars … or Will We? Feminism and Anti-Militarism, Where Next?" *Peace News* 247.

K, Laura. 2013. "Sports without War: Canada Out of Afghanistan, and Military Out of Sports," 15 August. http://www.wmtc.ca/2013/08/sports-without-war-canada-out-of.html.

Kane, Laura. 2016. "Trans Mountain Approval Prompts Anger in B.C." Canadian Press, 30 November.

Kelly, Cathal. 2014. "Baseball Players Wearing Camouflage? Make Sports, Not War." *Globe and Mail*, 26 May.

Keren, Michael. 2008. "A Canadian Alternative to the 'Clash of Civilizations.'" *International Journal of Canadian Studies* 37:41–55. https://doi.org/10.7202/040794ar.

Kingston, Anne. 2015. "Why Stephen Harper Doesn't Want to Talk about 'Women's Issues.'" *Maclean's*, 11 September. http://www.macleans.ca/politics/ottawa/why-stephen-harper-doesnt-want-to-talk-about-womens-issues/.

Knight, Amy. 1979. "Female Terrorists in the Russian Socialist Revolutionary Party." *Russian Review* 38 (2): 139–59. https://doi.org/10.2307/128603.

Koch, Klaus-Friedrich. 1974. *War and Peace in Jalémó*. Cambridge, MA: Harvard University Press. https://doi.org/10.4159/harvard.9780674181779.

Kuhn, Thomas S. 1962. *The Structure of Scientific Revolutions*. Chicago: University of Chicago Press.

Lévi-Strauss, Claude. (1949) 1969. *The Elementary Structures of Kinship*. Boston: Beacon.

Lewis, Bernard. 1990. "The Roots of Muslim Rage." *Atlantic Monthly* 266.

– 2002. *What Went Wrong? Western Impact and the Middle Eastern Response*. London: Phoenix.

Lewis, I.M. 1961. *A Pastoral Democracy: A Study of Pastoralism and Politics among the Northern Somali of the Horn of Africa*. Münster: LIT Verlag Münster.

Linden, Sidney B. 2007. *Report on the Ipperwash Inquiry*. Toronto: Publications Ontario.

Mackenzie, Lewis. 1993. *Peacekeeper: The Road to Sarajevo*. Vancouver: Douglas & McIntyre.

Malinowski, Bronislaw. (1922) 1961. *Argonauts of the Western Pacific*. New York: Dutton.

Mangan, J.A. 2006. "Sport and War: Combative Societies and Combative Sports." *SGI Quarterly*, July.

Mann, Spencer. 2014. "Harper v. First Nations: The Assimilation Agenda." IdelNoMore, 23 October. http://www.idlenomore.ca/harper_v_first_nations_the_assimilation_agenda.

Manuel, George, and Michael Posluns. 1974. *The Fourth World: An Indian Reality*. Toronto: Collier-Macmillan Canada.

Marshall, Tabitha. 2013. *Kelowna Accord*. Canadian Encyclopedia.

– 2014. "Oka Crisis." *Canadian Encyclopedia*, 15 July.

– 2016. "Ipperwash Crisis." *Canadian Encyclopedia*, 18 April.

Martel, Yann. 2001. *Life of Pi*. Orlando, FL: Harcourt.

Martin, Lawrence. 2010. *Harperland: The Politics of Control*. Toronto: Viking Canada.

– 2012. "Under This PM, the State Is Everywhere." *Globe and Mail*, 10 September.

McDonald, Marci. 2010. *The Armageddon Factor: The Rise of Christian Nationalism in Canada*. Toronto: Random House Canada.

McFate, Montgomery, and Andrea Jackson. 2005. "An Organizational Solution for DOD's Cultural Knowledge Needs." *Military Review* (July–August): 18–21.

McKay, Ian, and Jamie Swift. 2012. *Warrior Nation*. Toronto: Between the Lines.

McMurtry, John. 1971. "Kill 'Em! Crush 'Em! Eat 'Em Raw!" *Maclean's*, October.

– 1988. *Understanding War*. Canadian Papers in Peace Studies no. 2. Toronto: University of Toronto Press. Co-published 1989 by Science for Peace, Samuel Stevens, University of Toronto Press.

McQuaig, Linda. 2007. *Holding the Bully's Coat: Canada and the U.S. Empire*. Toronto: Doubleday Canada.

McSheffrey, Elizabeth. 2015. "Thank You, Stephen Harper, Sincerely, Indigenous Women." *National Observer*, 15 October.

Mead, Margaret. 1968. "Alternatives to War." In *War*, edited by Morton Fried, Marvin Harris, and Robert Murphy, 215–28. Garden City, NY: Natural History.

Melnyk, George. 2011. "Canada and Afghanistan: Peacemaking as Counterinsurgency Warfare. A Study in Political Rhetoric." *Peace Research* 43 (1): 5–29.

Melzer, Arthur M. 1996. "The Origin of the Counter-Enlightenment: Rousseau and the New Religion of Sincerity." *American Political Science Review* 90 (2): 344–60. https://doi.org/10.2307/2082889.

Nacos, Brigitte L. 2005. "The Portrayal of Female Terrorists in the Media." *Studies in Conflict and Terrorism* 28 (5): 435–51. https://doi.org/10.1080/10576100500180352.

Nadeau, Christian. 2011. *Rogue in Power*. Translated by Bob Chados, Eric Hamavitch, and Susan Jones. Toronto: James Lorimer.

Nadel, S.F. 1939. "The Interview Technique in Social Anthropology." In *The Study of Society: Methods and Problems*, edited by F.C. Bartlett et al., 317–27. New York: Macmillan.

National Defence. 2010. *Aboriginal People in the Canadian Military*. 29 January.

Needham, Rodney. 1973. *Right and Left: Essays on Dual Symbolic Classification*. Chicago: University of Chicago Press.

Nickerson, Michael. 2014. "Suffering Is Secondary." *Esprit de Corps* 21 (8): 24.

Nikiforuk, Andrew. 2010. *Tar Sands: Dirty Oil and the Future of a Continent*. Vancouver: Greystone Books.

Ontario. 2016. "The Algonquin Land Claim," 19 October.

Orwell, George. 1950. "The Sporting Spirit." In *Shooting an Elephant and Other Essays*, 151–5. New York: Harcourt, Brace and World.

Palmater, Pamela. 2015. "Harper's 10 Year War on First Nations." The Harper Decade. http://www.theharperdecade.com/blog/2015/7/14/harpers-10-year-war-on-first-nations.

Pearson, Lester B. 1955. *Democracy in World Politics*. Toronto: Princeton University Press and S.J. Reginald Saunders.

Price, David H. 2004. "Anthropologists as Spies." In *Anthropologists in the Public Sphere*, edited by R. González, 62–70. Austin: University of Texas Press.

– 2011. *Weaponizing Anthropology*. Oakland, CA: CounterPunch and AK.

Prystupa, Mychaylo. 2015. "How Harper Triggered a First Nations Legal War over Northern Gateway." *National Observer*, 1 October. https://www.nationalobserver.com/2015/10/01/news/how-harper-triggered-first-nations-legal-war-over-northern-gateway.

Radcliffe-Brown, A.R. 1922. *The Andaman Islanders*. Cambridge: Cambridge University Press.

Rae, Bob. 2015. *What's Happened to Politics?* Toronto: Simon and Schuster Canada.

Riches, David. 1986. *The Anthropology of Violence*. Oxford: Basil Blackwell.

Richler, Noah. 2012. *What We Talk About When We Talk About War*. Fredericton, NB: Goose Lane Editions.

Royal Commission on Aboriginal Peoples. 1996. *Report of the Royal Commission on Aboriginal Peoples*. Ottawa: Canada Communication Group.

Rubin, Alessa J., and Aurelien Breeden. 2016. "Women's Emergence as Terrorists in France Points to Shift in ISIS Gender Roles." *New York Times*, 1 October.

Runciman, David. 2015. "Fear in Those Blue Eyes." *London Review of Books* 37 (23): 5–10.

Russell, Bertrand. 1938. *Power: A New Social Analysis*. New York: W.W. Norton.

Said, Edward W. 2001. "The Clash of Ignorance." *Nation*, 22 October.

Salter, Mark B. 2003. "The Clash of Civilizations and the War on Terror(ists): An Imperialist Discourse." *Global Dialogue* 5 (1–2).

Sanders, Douglas E. 1977. "The Formation of the World Council of Indigenous Peoples." IWGIA document. www.iwgia.org/iwgia-files-publications-files/01823.29worldcouncil.pdf.

Sato, S. 1997. "The Clash of Civilizations: A View from Japan." *Asia-Pacific Review* 4 (2): 7–23.

Saul, John Ralston. 2014. *The Comeback*. Toronto: Penguin Canada.

Scott, James C. 1985. *Weapons of the Weak: Everyday Forms of Peasant Resistance*. New Haven, CT: Yale University Press.

Shaw, R. Paul, and Yuwa Wong. 1989. *Genetic Seeds of Warfare*. Boston: Unwin Hyman.

Shipley, Tyler. 2013. "The NHL and the New Canadian Militarism." *Canadian Dimension* 47 (4). https://canadiandimension.com/articles/view/the-nhl-and-the-new-canadian-militarism.

– 2014. "Exposing the Hypocrisy in Toronto Maple Leafs' 'Forces Appreciation Night.'" Rabble.ca, 10 February. http://rabble.ca/blogs/bloggers/views-expressed/2014/02/exposing-hypocrisy-toronto-maple-leafs-forces-appreciation-ni.

Simpson, Jeffrey. 2012. "First Nations Aren't Big Enough for True Sovereignty." *Globe and Mail*, 6 September.

Sims, Christopher J. 2015. *The Human Terrain System*. Carlisle, PA: U.S. Army War College Press.

Sinclair, Niigaan. 2014. "Idle No More: Where Is the Movement 2 Years Later?" CBC News, 7 December.

– 2015. "The White Paper, 1969." *Canadian Encyclopedia*.

Smith, Graeme. 2013. *The Dogs Are Eating Them Now: Our War in Afghanistan*. Toronto: Alfred A. Knopf Canada.

Staples, Steven. 2006. *Marching Orders*. A report commissioned by the Council of Canadians.

Stein, Janice Gross, and Eugene Lang. 2007. *The Unexpected War: Canada in Kandahar*. Toronto: Penguin Canada.

Steinson, Barbara J. 1980. "The Mother Half of Humanity." In *Women, War and Revolution*, edited by C. Berkin and C. Lovett, 259–81. Teaneck, NJ: Holmes and Meier.

Steward, Gillian. 2016. "Inquiry Must Look beyond Policing." *Toronto Star*, 23 August.

Stewart, Pamela J., and Andrew Strathern. 2002. *Violence: Theory and Ethnography*. London: Continuum.

Sun Tzu. (1910) 2009. *The Art of War*. Translated by Lionel Giles. Toronto: Prohyptikon Publishing.

Tasker, John Paul. 2016a. "Historic Land Deal with Algonquin Peoples Signed by Federal, Ontario Governments." CBC News, 18 October.

– 2016b. "Trudeau Cabinet Approves Trans Mountain, Line 3 Pipelines, Rejects Northern Gateway." CBC News, 29 November.

Turney-High, H.H. (1949) 1971. *Primitive War*. Columbia, SC: University of South Carolina Press.

Valpy, Michael. 2012. "Canada's Military: Invisible No More." *Globe and Mail*, 23 August.

Veterans Affairs Canada. 2014. "Canada Remembers Women in the Canadian Military." 8 December. www.veterans.gc.ca.

Weber, Max. 1949. *The Methodology of the Social Sciences*. Edited and translated by Edward A. Shils and Henry A. Finch. New York: Free Press.

Wells, Paul. 2013. *The Longer I'm Prime Minister: Stephen Harper and Canada, 2006–*. Toronto: Random House Canada.

"The White Paper 1969." First Nations and Indigenous Studies, University of British Columbia, 2009.

Whitworth, Sandra. 2005. "Militarized Masculinities and the Politics of Peacekeeping: The Canadian Case." In *Critical Security Studies in World Politics*, edited by Ken Booth, 89–106. Boulder, CO: Lynne Riemer Publishers.

Wilson, E.O. 1975. *Sociobiology: The New Synthesis*. Cambridge, MA: Belknap of Harvard University.

Winslow, Donna. 1997. *The Canadian Airborne Regiment in Somalia: A Socio-cultural Inquiry*. Ottawa: Minister of Public Works and Government Services Canada.

– 1999. "Rites of Passage and Group Bonding in the Canadian Airborne." *Armed Forces and Society* 25 (3): 429–57. https://doi.org/10.1177/009532 7X9902500305.

Zig Zag. 2007. "Oka Crisis, 1990." Warrior Publications. https://warriorpublications.wordpress.com/2014/06/11/oka-crisis-1990/.